FANTASTIC FONDUES

FANTASTIC FONDUES

HILAIRE WALDEN

PIATKUS

First published in 1996 by
Judy Piatkus (Publishers) Ltd
5 Windmill Street, London W1P 1HF

The moral right of the author has been asserted

*A catalogue record for this book is available from
the British Library*

ISBN 0-7499-1752-0

Designed by Suzanne Perkins Grafica
Illustrations by Madeleine David

Data capture by Intype London Ltd, London SW19
Printed and bound in Great Britain by
Mackays of Chatham PLC

Contents

Introduction

The word 'fondue' comes from the French *fondre*, 'to melt'. Fondues are traditionally associated with melted cheese and Switzerland, but there are also many meat, fish, vegetable and sweet ones from countries as far apart as France, the United States and China.

Fondues have a wonderfully relaxed air of informality, which breaks the ice at any gathering. A fondue party is an excellent idea for entertaining both old friends who are at ease with one another, and guests who are strangers; it is impossible to stand on ceremony when everyone is busy dipping pieces of food into the fondue pot.

In Switzerland, a fondue party is often an occasion for a great deal of hilarity and merriment. The test of a skilled fondue-eater is the dexterity and sureness with which he or she fixes the food on to their fork before plunging it into the gently bubbling fondue bowl. Anyone who drops a piece into the pot has to pay a forfeit. For a man, this is usually a bottle of wine; for a woman, a kiss or the promise of a fondue party at her home. At more racy gatherings, the penalty can be to remove an item of clothing.

I like to provide two or more different fondues, in different pots. They could be two different types of cheese fondue, or a cheese fondue and an oil or a stock or broth one, or a stock and oil fondue. When providing an oil or stock fondue I try to supply a variety of different foods to be cooked. With an oil one these could be Cheese Tempura (see page 68), Fondue-cooked Crisp-coated Courgette Chips (see page 66) and Shrimp Beignets (see page 72). For a stock fondue, they might be a selection of different wontons (see pages 34–42). And, of course, there would be plenty of dips, dipping sauces, salads, breads and other accompaniments such as good oil-cured black olives, gherkins, sun-dried tomatoes and toasted nuts.

Traditionally, a fondue is a meal in itself, perhaps with just some fresh fruit to follow, but this does not have to be the case. There's many a time that I have served a cheese, oil or stock fondue for a first course, with people eating less than they would if it had been the centre of the meal. I have also often served a

1

light first course before a fondue. And, of course, a dessert fondue can round off any meal.

EQUIPMENT

The type of fondue pot varies depending on the kind of fondue you are making.

Oil fondue pots

Fondue bourguignonne, tempuras and other fondues which involve deep-frying food at 180–190°C/350–375°F require a pot made of a material that will withstand high temperatures and transmit heat quickly to maintain the temperature even when cold food is being dipped. Copper lined with tin, or stainless steel, perhaps with a non-stick coating for easy cleaning, are the most suitable. The pot should be bulbous, with sides that slope inwards at the top to minimise hot oil splashes and help to hold in the heat. A lid is often included to cover the pot when guests are not dipping into the oil, or while the oil is being returned to the required temperature. Some pots have a ledge around the inside rim on which to hang the forks. Ideally, the handle of the pot should be short, to lessen the risk of accidents, but I have seen many fondue pots with handles that are as long as saucepan handles. Also for safety, the handle should be made of wood or some other heatproof material. Avoid pots with metal handles as they become impossibly hot with prolonged heating. A practical size for six to eight people would be about 9cm (3½ inches) deep with a base diameter of not more than 20cm (8 inches), and a capacity of about 1–1.5 litres (1¾–2½ pints). The pots may be used for cheese and dessert fondues provided the heat is kept low.

Oil fondues can also be cooked in saucepans or flameproof casseroles.

Cheese fondue pots

The temperature of a cheese fondue is lower than that of an oil one. Because the cheese has a tendency to stick, a thicker material that conducts heat more slowly is used, such as glazed earthenware or pottery, similar to the original Swiss *caquelon*, or enamelled cast-iron. Cheese fondue pots are wide and shallow and designed specifically to allow room for easy swirling of foods in the melted cheese mixture. One with a diameter of 18–20cm (7–8 inches) would be suitable for four to six people. Again, the handle should be short and of a heat-resistant material. If you don't have a special cheese fondue pot, you can just as easily use an enamelled cast-iron, or flameproof earthenware casserole. Do not attempt to use these pots for hot oil fondues.

Broth fondue pots

In Eastern countries a fondue pot called a steamboat or hotpot is used for stock or broth fondues. It is usually made of brass or copper with a tin lining. A lid with a funnel in the centre covers the pot, which contains hot stock into which morsels of food are dipped. The liquid is kept hot by glowing charcoal which is held in a small brazier beneath the pot. These pots are rather hard to find, but there is no reason why a stock fondue should not be cooked in an oil or cheese fondue pot, or a suitable saucepan or casserole.

Dessert fondue pots

You can use a cheese fondue pot, or an oil fondue pot, provided the heat is kept low. Small pots and a candle-burner are adequate for keeping the sauce hot.

Burners

The burner is one of the most important parts of a fondue set because it governs how well the set will work.

Methylated-spirit burners work on the same principle as an oil lamp. There is a reservoir holding the spirit, and either a wick or a compressed glass-wool pad. The heat is controlled by adjusting the length of the wick or the position of the burner cover. This has holes that can be opened or closed to regulate the supply of oxygen and govern the size of the flame. Meths burners tend to need practice before you can govern the flame effectively and they can be rather smelly.

Butane burners work in the same way as a camping stove. The container is filled with a pressurised pack of butane gas, and the heat is controlled by a knob on the outlet tube which is screwed in or out. These burners are easy to light and control and there is no smell. A butane pack may only be used in a fondue burner designed to hold it; there is no way you can swap if your fondue set has a meths burner.

Another alternative is to use small tablets of compressed combustible material held in a lidded container. The flame is simply controlled by adjusting the position of the lid.

Easiest of all are electric fondue pots which are thermostatically controlled to give the right heat for cheese, oil, stock or sweet fondues.

An electric plate-warmer can be brought into play for cheese fondues and dessert fondues, while an electric wok can be used for oil or stock ones.

Forks

Forks are usually supplied with a fondue set to enable the food to be dipped into the fondue. They should be at least 25 cm (10 inches) long with heatproof handles and long, sharp prongs. They are only intended for cooking the food in an oil fondue, not for eating it, because the prongs can become dangerously hot. Once cooked, the food is transferred to a dinner plate and eaten with an ordinary table fork.

Slotted spoon

A slotted spoon can sometimes come in handy for hot oil and stock fondues, for lifting the food from the pot. It can also be useful for removing crumbs or pieces of batter when cooking coated foods.

Chinese wire strainer

A Chinese wire strainer, available from Asian food and equipment shops and some specialist equipment shops, can be used in the same way as a slotted spoon.

Long chopsticks

These can be used for oriental fondues and wontons.

Fondue plates

Fondue plates made of china or glass, with several divisions for sauces and dips, are available. They sometimes come with a fondue set and the pot stands in the centre. A special fondue plate is not essential; you can use any dish with several compartments, or manage with small plates and bowls.

Heatproof table mat and tray
Hot drips may very quickly spoil the surface of a table-top, so it is a good idea to protect it with a cloth and heatproof mat. It is also best to stand the fondue set on a heatproof tray.

Absorbent paper towels
Have a good supply of absorbent paper towels for draining the food when you serve an oil fondue.

DRINKS

The same wine that is used to make the fondue is the best accompaniment to a cheese fondue. You can also serve some of the spirit used in the recipe: in Switzerland it is customary to have a chilled glass of kirsch half-way through the meal, as a digestive.

With oil and stock fondues I follow the usual wine-with-food maxim of red wine with red meats and white wine with fish and vegetables.

ORGANISING A FONDUE

The dips and sauces, and some of the salads, can usually be prepared beforehand, as can raw vegetable dippers if they are covered with cling film and kept cool. Other dippers, including meat and bread cubes, are best prepared as near as possible to the meal.

Place the fondue pot in the centre of the table. Arrange place settings of dinner plates, and 'eating' forks if serving an oil fondue, and put the fondue plate or the various plates and bowls of foods for dippers, dips, sauces, accompaniments, condiments, salads, etc. on the table. A plentiful supply of paper napkins can be invaluable, and if you are serving an oil fondue, line a large plate or shallow dish with the paper towels on which guests can drain their food, and have the roll of towels to hand.

About 15 minutes before the meal is due to start, light the fondue burner. This will ensure that it is burning properly when cooking starts.

Cheese Fondues

Cheese fondues originated in the mountainous Alpine regions of Switzerland where, in the winter months, snow often cut mountain-dwellers off from the world for months on end. Fondue was used to stretch food supplies until the roads were open again.

Traditionally, Swiss Gruyère or Emmental cheeses are used: they melt easily and have a good, definite flavour. Other cheeses can be substituted to make fondues with different characters and flavours. People's tastes vary, so you will have to experiment to find which ones you like.

An acid ingredient is often added. This is because it will help the cheese melt easily without going stringy. Originally in Switzerland, the acid in the young wine in which the cheese was melted would have been sufficient. Today, we often add a little lemon juice as well, depending on the melting qualities of the cheese, because wines have less acidity. Dry cider or beer is sometimes substituted for wine. The wine, cider or beer should be heated until it is almost boiling before the cheese is added.

To prevent the melted cheese from separating, cornflour can be added. Very little is needed – at most 1 tablespoon is enough for a fondue to serve four to six people. It is blended with a little liquid before being added to the cheese, then the mixture is stirred until it thickens slightly. The liquid is often a spirit such as kirsch or brandy, which not only contributes to the flavour of the fondue but seems to improve the texture.

The cheese will take about 4 minutes to melt. Keep stirring the cheese mixture in a figure-of-eight movement to prevent it becoming stringy and ensure that it is being heated evenly. Don't worry if the mixture forms a soft, dough-like ball in the centre of the liquor. This is quite normal and it gradually melts to form a smooth mixture. Whatever you do, do not be tempted to raise the heat and try to hurry the melting process along or you will over-cook and spoil the fondue. Throughout the cooking, it is essential to maintain a low heat.

Freshly ground black pepper, or occasionally other spices like nutmeg or paprika, is the only seasoning that should be needed; the cheese will provide sufficient salt.

Guests should be encouraged to swirl their pieces of bread in a deep figure-of-eight movement to keep the cheese mixture moving and prevent it sticking and burning. When most of the fondue has been eaten, the mixture at the base of the pot will have formed a crust: this is delicious and should be scraped out and shared among the guests. Should you still have any fondue left, it can be spread on pieces of firm bread the next day and toasted.

DIPPERS

The most important point about dippers is that they should be bite-sized.

Bread

Bread is the most widely used dipper. It should be firm; if it isn't, crumbs will dislodge or it will disintegrate when dipped through the cheese. If the bread is a little on the soft side, include some crust with each piece. It should be tasty. Be imaginative and offer a selection of different breads (see pages 127–137 for ideas), and perhaps include Corn and Chilli Mini Muffins (see page 128) or cubes of Parmesan Cake (see page 127). Providing a selection of more unusual breads is a good way of giving individuality to your fondue, and making yours the one people remember as being extra-special.

Cubes of bread can be topped with sun-dried tomatoes, pitted oil-cured black olives or pieces of anchovy fillet, before being speared on to a fork for extra-savoury mouthfuls. You can also spread the bread lightly with traditional or red pesto, *tapenade* (black olive and caper spread) or *anchoïade* (anchovy spread).

Vegetables

Vegetables make good dippers. Include a mixture – I like to serve some that are raw and some that are cooked – and for visual impact group them in their individual colours rather than mixing them up. I think cooked vegetables are better warm than cold, so that is the way I like to serve them – trying to remember to warm the dishes for them. I keep some of the cooked vegetables back so that they can be kept in a warm place for the later stages of the fondue. Of course, it is not always practical to serve warm, freshly cooked vegetables, but if you do cook them in advance, do this as near as possible to serving time and keep them at room temperature, not in the refrigerator.

Asparagus
The cooked stalks (not the tips because they are too soft) of fresh, slim asparagus that are not at all woody can be used. Also cooked, frozen stalks. Serve warm.

Aubergines
Choose small aubergines. Cut them into cubes, spread in a colander and sprinkle with salt. Leave for 30–60 minutes, then rinse well. Pat dry, then fry in hot olive oil until lightly browned and soft. Drain on paper towels. Serve warm.

Avocado
Use firm but ripe avocados. Just before serving, cut them into large cubes. Brush with just a little lemon juice, if liked.

Broccoli
Divide into small florets and serve either raw, or blanched in boiling water for 30–60 seconds. Drain and dry well. Serve warm.

Brussels sprouts
Cook small sprouts in boiling water until just tender. Drain and dry well. Serve warm.

Carrots
Avoid large, woody specimens. Cut into short lengths, cook in boiling salted water, then drain and dry well. Serve warm.

Cauliflower
Divide into small florets, blanch in boiling water for about 1 minute. Drain and dry well. Serve warm.

Celeriac
Cut into large cubes, then cook in boiling water until just tender. Drain and dry well.

Celery
Divide into individual sticks, and cut into short lengths.

Courgettes
Use small courgettes because they are firmer and have a better flavour. They can be served raw, or blanched for 30–60 seconds then drained and dried well.

Cucumber
Cut in half lengthways. Peel if liked, or opt for a compromise and remove strips of peel. Scoop out the seeds and cut the cucumber into bite-sized chunks.

Fennel
Can be served raw, or blanched for 30–60 seconds, then drained and refreshed under running cold water. Dry well.

Jerusalem artichokes
These are fiddly to peel, especially when raw, so cook them whole in boiling water until just tender. Drain, then peel them, and cut into largish cubes. Dry well. Serve warm.

Mushrooms
Choose chestnut or white cap mushrooms. Button mushrooms can be left whole but large ones should be cut into halves or quarters depending on size. Serve raw.

Parsnips
Avoid large, woody specimens. Cut into largish cubes, then cook in boiling water until just tender. Drain and dry well. Serve warm.

Peppers
Cut red peppers into smallish squares.

Potatoes
Cook new potatoes, halved if large, or chunks of salad or other waxy potatoes. On page 126 there is a recipe for Baked Potato Wedges. Serve warm.

Salsify
Scrub but do not peel. Cook whole in boiling water until just tender. Drain well, leave until cool enough to handle, then peel and cut into lengths. Serve warm.

Squash
For the best flavour and firmest texture, use butternut or kabocha squash, but other squashes, such as mini-patty-pan squashes in summer can be used (these are cooked whole). Peel the squash and cut into cubes, cook in boiling water until just tender, then drain well and refresh under running cold water. Dry well before serving.

Sweet potatoes
Cut into largish cubes, then cook in boiling water until just tender. Drain and dry well. Serve warm.

Tomatoes
Ripe cherry tomatoes make good dippers, but do warn your guests to take care when piercing them with the prongs of their forks or the seeds will spurt out.

Ham
Roll up strips of thinly sliced, cooked or cured ham such as Parma or Serrano.

Sausages
Cook British sausages and cut large ones into bite-sized pieces; chipolatas and cocktail sausages can be left whole. Continental cured sausages such as salamis, chorizo and frankfurters should be cut into chunks.

Prawns
Use peeled fresh or frozen cooked prawns.

Fruit
Fruits such as apples can provide a foil for the richness of a cheese fondue.

Apples and pears
Cut into thick slices or chunks and brush with lemon juice to prevent them discolouring.

Pineapple
Peel, cut into thickish slices and remove the cores. Cut into small chunks.

Classic Swiss Cheese Fondue

OF all the fondues I have served this is still the most popular.

1 clove garlic, halved lengthways

300ml (½ pint) medium-bodied dry white wine

3 tablespoons kirsch

1½ teaspoons cornflour

300g (10oz) Emmental cheese, grated

300g (10oz) Gruyère cheese, grated

freshly grated nutmeg

white pepper or paprika

selection of dippers (see page 7), to serve

1 Rub the cut sides of the garlic around the inside of a fondue pot.

2 Pour the wine into the pot and heat gently, uncovered, until bubbles begin to appear.

3 Stir the kirsch into the cornflour until smooth.

4 Add the cheeses to the wine and stir constantly in a figure-of-eight movement over a very low heat until the cheeses have melted and the mixture is just beginning to bubble around the edges – about 4 minutes. Continue to stir until the mixture is smooth.

5 Stir the kirsch and cornflour mixture into the fondue and continue to heat, stirring, until the fondue is smooth and thickened – about 2–3 minutes. Do not allow to boil.

6 Season to taste with freshly grated nutmeg and white pepper or paprika, and serve with your choice of dippers.

Herby Cheese Fondue

*T*HIS is a good fondue to serve in summer when the flavour of the herbs is at its best.

SERVES 4

1 clove garlic, halved lengthways

175ml (6fl oz) dry white wine

1 teaspoon lemon juice

3 tablespoons kirsch

2 teaspoons cornflour

225g (½lb) mature Gouda cheese, or Emmental cheese, grated

225g (½lb) Gruyère cheese, grated

leaves from a small bunch of tarragon, chopped

1–2 tablespoons chopped parsley

freshly ground black pepper

selection of dippers (see page 7), to serve

---

1 Rub the cut sides of the garlic around the inside of a fondue pot.

2 Pour the wine and lemon juice into the pot and heat gently, uncovered, until bubbles begin to appear.

3 Stir the kirsch into the cornflour until smooth.

4 Add the cheeses, and stir in a figure-of-eight movement over a very low heat until the mixture is just beginning to bubble at the edges – about 4 minutes.

5 Stir the kirsch and cornflour mixture and the herbs into the fondue and heat, stirring, until the fondue is smooth and thickened – about 2–3 minutes. Do not allow to boil.

6 Season to taste with pepper, and serve with your choice of dippers.

Italian Cheese Fondue

THREE Italian cheeses with good melting and cooking qualities make this one of my favourite fondues.

SERVES 4

1 clove garlic, halved lengthways

225ml (8fl oz) dry white wine

2 teaspoons lemon juice

225g (½lb) mozzarella cheese, grated

225g (½lb) fontina cheese, grated

75g (3oz) Parmesan cheese, freshly grated

50ml (2fl oz) milk

2 teaspoons cornflour

freshly ground black pepper

selection of dippers (see page 7), to serve

1 Rub the cut sides of the garlic around the inside of a fondue pot.

2 Pour in the wine and lemon juice and heat gently, uncovered, until bubbles begin to appear.

3 Add the cheeses and stir in a figure-of-eight movement over a very low heat until the cheeses have melted and the mixture is just beginning to bubble at the edges – about 4 minutes.

4 Blend the milk into the cornflour until smooth.

5 Stir the milk and cornflour mixture into the fondue and heat, stirring constantly, until the fondue is smooth and thickened – about 2–3 minutes. Do not allow to boil.

6 Season to taste with pepper and serve with your choice of dippers.

VARIATIONS
Add pieces of coarsely chopped oil-cured black olives, sun-dried tomatoes or cooked vegetables, such as grilled artichoke hearts and grilled mushrooms, that have been packed in oil.

Smoked-Cheese Fondue

*A*PPLE wedges, chunks of frankfurter sausage, rye bread and caraway bread are appropriate accompaniments for this fondue.

SERVES 4

½ small onion

225ml (8fl oz) lager

2 teaspoons lemon juice

350g (12oz) smoked cheese, grated

175g (6oz) Emmental cheese, grated

3 tablespoons milk

2 teaspoons cornflour

2–3 teaspoons German mustard, to taste

1 Rub the cut side of the onion around the inside of a fondue pot.

2 Pour the lager and lemon juice into the pot and heat gently, uncovered, until almost boiling.

3 Add the cheeses and stir in a figure-of-eight movement over a very low heat until the cheeses have melted and the mixture is just beginning to bubble at the edges – about 4 minutes.

4 Blend the milk into the cornflour and mustard until smooth.

5 Stir the mixture into the fondue and heat, stirring constantly, until the fondue is smooth and thickened – about 2–3 minutes. Do not allow to boil.

Creamy Blue-Cheese Fondue

*T*HIS is a good way to use up odds and ends of blue cheese that are still perfectly edible; do not use them, though, if it is a choice between the fondue pot and the waste bin. You can alter the ratio of blue cheese to cream cheese according to its pungency and your taste. About 2 tablespoons of chopped parsley, chives, thyme, basil or rosemary (very finely chopped) is a good addition.

SERVES 3–4

1 clove garlic, halved lengthways

175g (6oz) full-fat soft cheese

225ml (8fl oz) milk

300g (10oz) creamy blue cheese such as Stilton or Gorgonzola, grated or finely crumbled

2 tablespoons crème fraîche

1 tablespoon cornflour

freshly ground black pepper

selection of dippers (see page 7), to serve

1 Rub the cut sides of the garlic around the inside of a fondue pot.

2 Put the soft cheese into the pot, then gradually add the milk, beating until smooth.

3 Heat gently until thoroughly warmed, then add the blue cheese. Stir in a figure-of-eight movement over a very low heat until the cheese has melted and the mixture is just beginning to bubble at the edges – about 4 minutes.

4 Stir the crème fraîche into the cornflour until smooth.

5 Stir the mixture into the fondue and heat, stirring constantly, until the fondue is smooth and thickened – about 2–3 minutes. Do not allow to boil. Season to taste with pepper and serve with your choice of dippers.

West Country Fondue

◖

SERVE this as a fondue variation of a ploughman's lunch, accompanying it with thick apple slices, pickles and pickled onions. You could add some chutney to the fondue.

SERVES 4

250ml (9fl oz) dry cider
2 teaspoons lemon juice
450g (1lb) mature Cheddar cheese, grated
2 tablespoons kirsch or brandy

2 teaspoons cornflour
1–2 tablespoons Dijon mustard, to taste
freshly ground black pepper

1 Pour the cider and lemon juice into a saucepan and heat gently, uncovered, until almost boiling.

2 Add the cheese and stir in a figure-of-eight movement over a very low heat until the cheese has melted and the mixture is just beginning to bubble at the edges – about 4 minutes.

3 Stir the kirsch or brandy into the cornflour and mustard to make a smooth paste.

4 Stir the paste into the fondue and heat, stirring constantly, until the fondue is smooth and thickened – about 2–3 minutes. Do not allow to boil. Season with pepper and adjust the level of mustard, if necessary.

5 To serve, pour the fondue into a warmed fondue pot and put over a burner. Heat gently, stirring, until the fondue is warmed through.

Camembert Fondue

I combine Gruyère cheese with the Camembert to give the fondue more 'body'.

SERVES 4

1 clove garlic, halved

225ml (8fl oz) medium-bodied dry white wine

1 teaspoon lemon juice

350g (12oz) Camembert cheese, rind removed, chopped

150g (5oz) Gruyère cheese, grated

2 tablespoons single cream

2 teaspoons cornflour

3 tablespoons Calvados or brandy

freshly ground black pepper

selection of dippers (see page 7), to serve

1 Rub the cut sides of the garlic around the inside of a fondue pot.

2 Pour the wine and lemon juice into the pot and heat gently, uncovered, until bubbles begin to appear.

3 Add the cheeses and stir in a figure-of-eight movement over a very low heat until the cheeses have melted and the mixture is just beginning to bubble at the edges – about 4 minutes.

4 Stir the cream into the cornflour to make a smooth paste. Stir the paste into the fondue and heat, stirring constantly, until the fondue is smooth and thickened – about 2–3 minutes. Do not allow to boil. Add the Calvados or brandy and season with pepper. Serve with your choice of dippers.

Dutch Fondue

*I*N Holland, many years ago, farmers' wives used to make fondues from cheeses that were not of a good enough shape to send to market. Dutch gin adds a distinctive flavour, but use ordinary gin if you cannot find it. I've used gin in other fondue recipes when I've run out of kirsch and they are always extremely popular. If you come across Gouda with cumin seeds, try that.

SERVES 4

1 clove garlic, halved lengthways

150ml (5fl oz) dry white wine

1 teaspoon lemon juice

400g (14oz) mature Gouda cheese, grated

2 tablespoons Dutch gin or ordinary gin

2 teaspoons cornflour

freshly ground black pepper

selection of dippers (see page 7), to serve

1 Rub the cut sides of the garlic around the inside of a fondue pot.

2 Pour the wine and lemon juice into the pot and heat gently, uncovered, until bubbles begin to appear.

3 Add the cheese and stir in a figure-of-eight movement over a very low heat until it has melted and the mixture is just beginning to bubble at the edges – about 4 minutes.

4 Stir the gin into the cornflour until smooth.

5 Stir the gin and cornflour mixture into the fondue and heat, stirring constantly, until the fondue is smooth and thickened. Do not allow to boil. Season with pepper and serve with your choice of dippers.

Cheese and Tomato Fondue

FLAVOURED with tomato and herbs, this is one of my most popular fondues.

SERVES 3–4

---

1 clove garlic, halved lengthways

40g (1½oz) salted butter

4 well-flavoured tomatoes, peeled, seeded and chopped

½ teaspoon dried oregano

½ teaspoon paprika

175ml (6fl oz) dry white wine

450g (1lb) mature Cheddar cheese, grated

1 tablespoon chopped basil

freshly ground black pepper

selection of dippers (see page 7), to serve

---

1 Rub the cut sides of the garlic around the inside of a fondue pot. Add the butter and heat until melted.

2 Add the tomatoes and oregano. Cook, stirring occasionally, for 6–8 minutes, then stir in the paprika for 1 minute.

3 Add the wine and heat gently, uncovered, until it begins to bubble, then gradually add the cheese, stirring in a figure-of-eight movement over a very low heat until it has melted and the fondue is smooth, thick and creamy.

4 Add the basil and season with pepper. Serve with your choice of dippers.

Cheese and Onion Fondue

*O*NION, gently fried until tender and sweet, gives an extra dimension to a cheese fondue. The cooking of the onion can be done in advance.

SERVES 4

40g (1½oz) butter

1 large onion, finely chopped

225ml (8fl oz) dry white wine

300g (10oz) mature Cheddar cheese, grated

300g (10oz) Gruyère cheese, grated

2 teaspoons cornflour

2-3 teaspoons chopped chives

1-2 tablespoons Dijon mustard, to taste

freshly ground black pepper

selection of dippers (see page 7), to serve

1 Heat the butter in a saucepan, add the onion and cook gently until softened and buttery but not coloured.

2 Pour in most of the wine and heat, uncovered, until bubbles begin to appear. Cover, remove from the heat and leave to infuse for 30 minutes.

3 Return the pan to the heat and heat, uncovered, until the wine is almost boiling.

4 Add the cheeses and stir in a figure-of-eight movement over a very low heat until the cheeses have melted and the mixture is beginning to bubble around the edges – about 4 minutes.

5 Blend the remaining wine into the cornflour to make a smooth paste.

6 Stir the paste into the fondue and heat, stirring constantly, until the fondue is smooth and thickened – about 2-3 minutes. Do not allow to boil. Add the chives, and mustard and pepper to taste. Serve with your choice of dippers.

7 To serve, pour the fondue into a warmed pot and put over a burner. Heat gently, stirring, until the fondue is warmed through.

Cauliflower Cheese Fondue

THIS fondue is based on a cheese sauce, so is more economical and less rich than a traditional one. Other dippers apart from, or as well as cauliflower, can be used, such as Walnut Bread (see page 136), Sun-dried Tomato and Basil Focaccia (see page 134), Spiced Breadsticks (see page 133), Herb Bread (see page 131) and Corn and Chilli Mini Muffins (see page 128).

──────────────── SERVES 4–6 ────────────────

40g (1½oz) butter

40g (1½oz) plain flour

570ml (1 pint) milk

1–2 egg yolks (large)

175g (6oz) Gruyère cheese, grated

40g (1½oz) freshly grated Parmesan cheese

1½–2 tablespoons wholegrain mustard, to taste

salt and freshly ground black pepper

blanched cauliflower florets, to serve

1 Heat the butter in a heavy-based saucepan, preferably non-stick, then stir in the flour for 1–2 minutes. Draw the pan from the heat and slowly pour in the milk, stirring. Return the pan to the heat and continue to stir until the sauce boils and thickens. Leave to simmer for 3–4 minutes, stirring occasionally, to cook the flour so preventing a raw-flour taste.

2 Remove the pan from the heat and immediately stir in the egg yolk(s) and cheeses until the cheeses have melted. Add mustard and seasoning to taste; very little salt should be needed.

3 To serve, pour the sauce into a warmed fondue pot and put over a burner.

4 Heat gently, stirring, until the fondue is warmed through. Serve with the cauliflower florets.

Cheddar and Beer Fondue

*F*OR the best results do, please, use a mature cheese, preferably one from a traditional farmhouse cheesemaker. This is not only because the flavour will be so much better, but the texture and consistency of immature cheese is not conducive to making the best fondues.

SERVES 4

300ml (½ pint) beer

2 teaspoons lemon juice

450g (1lb) mature Cheddar cheese, grated

2 teaspoons cornflour

½ teaspoon English mustard powder

2 tablespoons whisky or brandy

freshly ground black pepper or paprika (optional)

selection of dippers (see page 7), to serve

1 Pour the beer and lemon juice into a fondue pot and heat gently, uncovered, until bubbles begin to appear.

2 Add the cheese and stir constantly in a figure-of-eight movement over a very low heat until the cheese has melted and the mixture is just beginning to bubble at the edges – about 4 minutes.

3 Mix the cornflour, mustard powder and whisky or brandy to a smooth paste.

4 Stir the paste into the fondue and heat, stirring constantly, until the mixture is smooth and thickened – about 2–3 minutes. Do not allow to boil. Season with pepper or paprika, if liked, and serve with your choice of dippers.

Apple and Cheese Fondue

UNSWEETENED apple juice takes the place of wine in this fondue, and gives a more fruity, winey flavour to Cheddar cheese. As well as apple slices, I include celery among the dippers.

SERVES 6

1 clove garlic, halved lengthways

450ml (15fl oz) unsweetened apple juice

1 tablespoon cornflour

¼ teaspoon English mustard powder

¼ teaspoon paprika

1 tablespoon lemon juice

700g (1½lb) mature Cheddar cheese, grated

4–5 eating apples, peeled, cored, cubed and tossed in lemon juice, to serve

1 Rub the cut sides of the garlic around the inside of a fondue pot.

2 Stir enough apple juice into the cornflour, mustard and paprika to make a smooth paste.

3 Pour the remaining apple juice and the lemon juice into the fondue pot and heat gently, uncovered, until bubbles begin to appear.

4 Add the cheese and stir in a figure-of-eight movement over a very low heat until the cheese has melted and the mixture is just beginning to bubble at the edges – about 5–6 minutes.

5 Stir in the cornflour paste and bring slowly to the boil, stirring until smooth and thickened – about 2–3 minutes. Do not overcook or the mixture will curdle and separate. Serve with the apple slices.

Devilled Cheese Fondue

ADJUST the levels of the flavourings according to whether you want a subtly different flavour or a fondue with a definitely different taste.

—————————— SERVES 4 ——————————

1 clove garlic, halved lengthways

225ml (8fl oz) dry white wine

225g (8oz) mature Cheddar cheese, grated

350g (12oz) Gruyère cheese, grated

2 tablespoons gin

2 teaspoons cornflour

2-3 teaspoons Worcestershire sauce

1-2 teaspoons horseradish relish

1 teaspoon paprika

freshly ground black pepper

selection of dippers (see page 7), to serve

1 Rub the cut sides of the garlic around the inside of a fondue pot.

2 Pour the wine into the fondue pot and heat gently, uncovered, until bubbles begin to appear.

3 Add the cheeses and stir in a figure-of-eight movement over a very low heat until the cheeses have melted and the mixture is just beginning to bubble at the edges – about 4 minutes.

4 Stir the gin into the cornflour until smooth, then stir this into the fondue and heat, stirring constantly until the mixture is smooth and thickened – about 2–3 minutes. Do not allow to boil. Add Worcestershire sauce, horseradish relish, paprika and plenty of pepper, to taste, and serve with your choice of dippers.

Fonduta

*F*ONDUTA is the Italian version of fondue, and comes from the Piedmont region which uses the local fontina cheese from the Val d'Aosta. It is a wonderful cheese for cooking because it melts beautifully. The classic Fonduta includes thin slices of white Alba truffle, which are added after the fondue has been prepared.

SERVES 4

400g (14oz) fontina cheese, cubed

300ml (½ pint) milk

25g (1oz) unsalted butter

4 eggs, beaten

freshly ground black pepper

selection of dippers (see page 7), to serve

1 Soak the cheese in the milk for at least 4 hours; the milk should just cover the cheese.

2 Melt the butter in a double boiler or a heatproof bowl set over a saucepan of simmering water, and add the eggs, the cheese and a little of the milk that has not been absorbed by the cheese. Cook gently, stirring, until the cheese has melted and the mixture is smooth, with the consistency of thick cream. Season with pepper.

3 Pour into a warmed fondue pot, put over a burner and serve with your choice of dippers.

Curried Cheese Fondue

USE your favourite curry paste – mild, medium, hot or spicy Indian, or red or green Thai paste – in the amount to achieve the effect you want. Naan Bread (see page 135) is an obvious choice to include among the dippers.

SERVES 4

1 clove garlic, halved lengthways

about 3 teaspoons curry paste, to taste

225ml (8fl oz) dry white wine

1½ teaspoons lemon juice

225g (8oz) mature Cheddar cheese, grated

300g (10oz) Gruyère cheese, grated

3 tablespoons milk

1½ teaspoons cornflour

freshly ground black pepper

selection of dippers (see above and page 7), to serve

1 Rub the cut sides of the garlic around the inside of a fondue pot. Add the curry paste to the pot, then stir in the wine and lemon juice. Heat gently, uncovered, until bubbles begin to appear.

2 Stir the cheeses into the fondue pot and stir in a figure-of-eight movement over a very low heat until the cheeses have melted and the mixture is just beginning to bubble at the edges – about 4 minutes.

3 Stir the milk into the cornflour until evenly blended. Stir this into the fondue and heat, stirring constantly, until the mixture is smooth and thickened – about 2–3 minutes. Do not allow to boil. Season to taste with pepper and add more curry paste if necessary. Serve with a selection of dippers.

VARIATION
Tandoori Cheese Fondue
Use tandoori paste instead of curry paste.

Microwave Cheese Fondue

MAKE sure the dish you choose will be suitable for heating over a fondue burner.

175ml (6fl oz) dry white wine

350g (12oz) Gruyère cheese, grated

2–3 teaspoons wholegrain mustard

115g (4oz) full-fat soft cheese with chives

selection of dippers (see page 7), to serve

1 Put the wine, Gruyère, mustard and soft cheese in a 1.25 litre (2 pint) microwave-proof casserole. Cook on 100% power (HIGH) for about 5 minutes until the cheeses have melted and the fondue is bubbling; stir every minute.

2 Put over a fondue burner. Serve with your choice of dippers.

Stock Fondues

Cooking foods in a stock or broth is a healthy way of eating, and if you are serving meat, especially, its flavour will infuse the liquid. This can be served as the most wonderful soup, enhanced, perhaps, by a dash or so of sherry or Madeira.

The fondue pot is usually filled about two-thirds full of stock or broth: the more liquid there is, the less the temperature will be lowered when cold food is added – but if the pot contains too much liquid, it will overflow when the food is put in.

The liquid must be simmering when meat or fish is added, boiling for vegetables, and this should be maintained throughout the cooking.

As with cheese fondues, the foods for dipping should be cut into bite-sized pieces. It is preferable to have food that won't take too long to cook, so choose prime, tender cuts of meat, fish and quick-cooking vegetables.

The broth or stock fondues that are found across South-East Asia and China go under such names as Mongolian hotpot and 'dip-dips' and contain various combinations of meat, poultry, bean curd, vegetables and noodles. To use the traditional hotpot or steamboat, place it on a heatproof surface and put unlit charcoal in its central chimney 15–20 minutes before the meal is due to start. Pour the stock or broth into the 'moat' that surrounds the chimney, ignite the charcoal and leave it to become really hot, causing the liquid to boil. (Do not light the charcoal before there is liquid in the moat as the heat will melt the sealing parts of the pot.)

Arrange all the different elements – meats, fish, individual vegetables, noodles, dips, sauces and other accompaniments – in separate bowls and place them around the hotpot. I like to make two separate sets of bowls to save guests stretching to reach what they want, or having to ask other guests, who may be engrossed in a fascinating conversation, to pass it. Supply each guest with a plate, chopsticks and/or a fondue fork, a soup spoon and a small bowl for their dipping sauce. Everyone puts spoonfuls of the sauce into their small bowls and adds any additional flavourings they fancy. This can also be done as the meal progresses. I provide a basic 'master sauce' to give people a starting-point.

Everyone uses chopsticks or a fondue fork to dip pieces of meat or fish into the boiling stock until cooked to taste, then dips them into the sauce before eating them. When guests have eaten all the meat and fish they want, the vegetables and bean curd are added to the pot as required, and cooked only long enough to heat through. They are eaten, like the meat, by dipping them first in the sauce. Noodles can now be heated in the pot. However, because of the difficulty of fishing them out with forks or chopsticks, I prefer to heat them by putting them separately in a bowl of boiling water, then draining them and adding them to guests' individual sauce bowls. When the noodles have been eaten, the liquid, which will now be infused with all the flavours of the other ingredients, is poured into the sauce bowls, mixed with any sauce that is left, and drunk as a soup.

Fish Stock

*W*HENEVER you buy fresh fish ask the fishmonger for some fish skin, trimmings and bones, and prawn or crab shells, for making fish stock. (A conical strainer comes in really useful when straining stocks.) If you do not need any fish stock at the time, freeze it so that it is to hand when you do need it.

1 onion, sliced
1 carrot, sliced
1 celery stick, sliced
fish and shellfish trimmings and bones
fennel trimmings and mushroom stalks,
   if available

100ml (3½fl oz) medium-bodied dry
   white wine
a small handful of parsley stalks
1 bay leaf
a few sprigs of fresh thyme
4 white peppercorns, lightly crushed

1 Put all the ingredients into a saucepan, add enough water to cover and bring to the boil.

2 Remove the scum from the surface and simmer the stock for about 20 minutes.

3 Strain the stock through a double layer of muslin and leave to cool. Remove any fat from the surface and store in the refrigerator for up to 2 days, or freeze.

Vegetable Stock

PREPARE a batch or two of real vegetable stock when you have just a little time and keep in the refrigerator or freezer for instantly adding distinction to sauces, soups and casseroles.

2 tablespoons oil	4 celery sticks, chopped
1 onion, finely chopped	vegetable trimmings such as celery and fennel tops, mushroom stalks and tomato skins and seeds
1 carrot, diced	
1 leek, sliced	
50g (2oz) young turnip, diced	1 fresh bouquet garni
50g (2oz) parsnip, diced	6 black peppercorns, lightly crushed

1 Heat the oil in a saucepan, add the onion and fry gently for about 5 minutes, or until soft and lightly coloured.

2 Add the other vegetables to the pan, with the trimmings, bouquet garni and peppercorns, and cover with cold water.

3 Bring to the boil, partially cover the pan, and simmer for 30 minutes, skimming occasionally. If you want the stock to be reduced further, boil it down after straining it.

4 Strain the stock and leave to cool. Cover and store in the refrigerator for up to 2 days, or freeze.

Chicken Stock

A supply of good home-made chicken stock is invaluable (it freezes excellently). It is not time-consuming to prepare and requires hardly any attention while cooking, but takes just a little longer than other stocks to cook. Lamb or veal bones can be substituted for the chicken to make a meat stock.

---

1 chicken carcass, bones and trimmings from a roast chicken

1 onion, sliced

1 carrot, sliced

1 leek, sliced

1 celery stick, sliced

vegetable trimmings such as mushroom stalks, celery leaves, fennel leaves

1 fresh bouquet garni

1 bay leaf

6 black peppercorns, lightly crushed

---

1 Break up the carcass and put in a large saucepan, with any skin and meat attached, plus other bones and trimmings.

2 Add the onion, carrot, leek, celery, vegetable trimmings, bouquet garni, bay leaf and peppercorns. Cover with cold water and bring to the boil. Skim the surface, partially cover the saucepan, and simmer for 2–3 hours, skimming the surface occasionally.

3 Strain the stock, leave to cool, then remove all traces of fat.

4 Store in the refrigerator, reboiling every other day, or freeze.

Fondue with Mediterranean Wontons

*T*HE filling can be made the day before and kept, covered, in the refrigerator, but do not fill the wonton wrappers until shortly before they are required because the moisture in the filling will dissolve the dough. Most of the dips, sauces and salads in the book can be served as accompaniments.

================ SERVES 4–6 ================

about 24 wonton wrappers

flour, for dusting

FILLING

2 tablespoons olive oil

2 shallots, finely chopped

1 clove garlic, crushed and finely chopped

1 red pepper, cut into 5mm (¼ inch) dice

1 yellow pepper, cut into 5mm (¼ inch) dice

2 egg yolks, beaten, for brushing

chicken or vegetable stock (see pages 32 and 33), for poaching

1 courgette (about 115g/4oz), cut into 5mm (¼ inch) dice

115g (4oz) soft goats' cheese, crumbled

2 tablespoons chopped coriander or parsley

12 oil-cured black olives, pitted and chopped

salt and freshly ground black pepper

1 To make the filling, heat the oil in a frying pan, add the shallots, garlic, peppers and courgette and fry for 4 minutes. Tip into a colander and leave to drain.

2 Mix the fried vegetables with the remaining filling ingredients.

3 Spread out a wonton wrapper on a lightly floured surface and brush the edges with beaten egg. Put a heaped teaspoon of the filling in the centre and fold over the corners to meet in the centre. Press the edges firmly together to seal. Repeat with the remaining wrappers and filling.

4 To serve, heat enough stock to two-thirds fill a fondue pot in a saucepan on the hob until it boils. Pour into the warmed fondue pot and put over a burner. Heat to simmering point and poach the wontons in batches for about 1 minute. They will sink at first, then rise to the surface after about 30 seconds; nudge free any that stick to the bottom. Keep more stock warm on the hob.

5 Remove the wontons with a Chinese wire strainer or slotted spoon.

Oriental Fondue with a Duo of Scallops

*T*HIS is a sophisticated fondue and needs two fondue or other pots: a metal one for deep-frying the succulent scallop meat fritters, and an earthenware or cast-iron one for poaching the delicate scallop-coral parcels. You can serve both types at the same time, or serve one before the other. I suggest the coral parcels first – cook them first if you decide to do this.

Kelp is sometimes sold as konbu or kombu. The stock can be made in advance up to the end of step 2.

SERVES 4

25g (1oz) kelp
1.1 litres (2 pints) cold water

25g (1oz) dried bonito flakes
1 tablespoon soy sauce
Hot Sweet and Sour Dipping Sauce (see page 104), to serve

CORAL PARCELS

coral from the 8 scallops used for the fritters below
1 clove garlic, chopped
2.5cm (1 inch) piece of ginger, grated
1 teaspoon soy sauce
1 teaspoon fish sauce
50g (2oz) tofu

12 wonton wrappers
flour, for dusting
1 red chilli, seeded and finely sliced (optional)
1 spring onion, finely sliced
12 coriander leaves

SCALLOP FRITTERS

8 scallops, corals reserved for the parcels above
1 sheet of nori, cut into 8 strips
Lager Batter (see page 61)

oil for deep frying

1 Put the kelp and water in a medium saucepan and simmer, without allowing the water to boil, until the kelp is soft and the stock is strong enough. Discard the kelp.

2 Add 150ml (5fl oz) cold water and the bonito flakes to the pan and bring to the boil. Strain through muslin or a clean tea-towel, and add the soy sauce.

3 To make the coral parcels, put the first six ingredients in a blender or food processor and mix until smooth.

4 Spread out a wonton wrapper on a lightly floured surface and put ½ teaspoon of the coral mixture in the centre. Top the filling with a slice of chilli, if liked, 2 slices of spring onion and a coriander leaf. Moisten the edges of the wrapper with water and either fold them up to make a purse shape, or fold them over the filling. Seal the edges. Repeat with the remaining wrappers and filling.

5 To make the fritters, wrap each scallop in a strip of nori.

6 To serve, heat enough oil to half-fill a fondue pot in a saucepan on the hob to 190°C/375°F. Carefully pour into the warmed fondue pot and put over a burner. Dip the wrapped scallops into the Lager Batter and deep-fry for about 3 minutes. Remove with a slotted spoon or Chinese wire strainer and drain on paper towels.

7 Meanwhile, reheat enough stock to two-thirds fill a fondue pot in a saucepan on the hob, then pour into the warmed fondue pot. Put over a burner, heat to simmering point and poach the coral parcels for about 3 minutes. They will sink to the bottom at first, then rise to the surface; nudge free any that stick to the bottom. Remove with a Chinese wire strainer or slotted spoon. Serve the parcels and fritters with the Hot Sweet and Sour Dipping Sauce. Keep more stock warm on the hob.

East-West Fondue with Cheese and Herb Wontons

❧

*T*HESE delicate filled 'dumplings' have elements of Eastern and Western cooking. The filling can be made a day in advance, but do not fill the wrappers until just before cooking. Serve with your choice of dips, sauces and other accompaniments.

SERVES 4–6

about 24 wonton wrappers

flour, for dusting

2 eggs, beaten, for brushing

FILLING

115g (4oz) soft mild goats' cheese

115g (4oz) Ricotta cheese

3 tablespoons finely chopped white part of spring onion

chicken or vegetable stock (see pages 33 and 32), for poaching

a handful of coriander

a handful of parsley

2 tablespoons finely chopped chives

1½ teaspoons finely chopped coriander

salt and freshly ground black pepper

1 To make the filling, mix all the ingredients together.

2 Spread out a wonton wrapper on a lightly floured surface and brush the edges with egg. Put a heaped teaspoon of filling in the centre and fold up the edges to enclose it. Press the edges together firmly. Repeat with the remaining wrappers and filling.

3 To serve, pour enough stock to two-thirds fill a fondue pot into a saucepan and simmer on the hob with the coriander and parsley for 5–10 minutes. Pour into the warmed fondue pot and put over a burner.

4 Heat to simmering point and poach the wontons in batches for about 1 minute – they will sink at first, then rise to the surface after about 30 seconds; nudge free any that stick to the bottom. Remove the wantons with a Chinese wire strainer or slotted spoon. Keep more stock warm on the hob.

Thai-Flavoured Fish Fondue with Salmon Wontons

*I*NSTEAD of salmon you could use the same amount of crabmeat, or 175g (6oz) peeled prawns.

SERVES 4–6

175–225g (6–8oz) salmon, skinned	1 teaspoon rice vinegar
2cm (¾ inch) piece of ginger, grated	½ teaspoon fish or oyster sauce
3 spring onions, finely chopped	24 wonton wrappers
50g (2oz) bean sprouts, chopped	flour, for dusting
1 clove garlic, finely crushed	fish stock (see page 31), for poaching
1 tablespoon soy sauce	3 stalks of lemon grass, bruised
1 teaspoon sesame oil	a walnut-sized piece of ginger, bruised

1 Make sure all the bones have been removed from the salmon, then, using a very sharp knife, chop it into fine dice; do not use a food processor as this tends to reduce the salmon to a paste.

2 Mix the salmon with the grated ginger, spring onions, bean sprouts, garlic, soy sauce, oil, vinegar and fish or oyster sauce.

3 Spread out a wonton wrapper on a lightly floured surface and moisten the edges with water. Place a teaspoon of filling in the centre and fold up the edges to enclose it. Press the edges firmly together. Repeat with the remaining filling and wonton wrappers.

4 To serve, pour enough stock to two-thirds fill a fondue pot into a saucepan, add the lemon grass and ginger and bring to the boil on the hob. Pour into the warmed fondue pot and put over a burner. Keep more stock warm on the hob. Heat to simmering point and poach the wontons in batches for 2–3 minutes. They will sink to the bottom at first, then rise to the surface; nudge free any that stick to the bottom. Remove with a Chinese wire strainer or slotted spoon and serve with your choice of accompaniments.

Fondue with Pink Trout Balls and Mustard Dill Dip

GARNISH the dish of uncooked trout balls with sprigs of dill and lemon wedges.

SERVES 4

225–300g (8–10oz) pink trout fillets, skinned

2 tablespoons crème fraîche

1 large egg white

finely grated rind of 1 lemon

a few drops of Tabasco sauce

salt

fish stock (see page 00), for cooking

MUSTARD AND DILL DIP

4 tablespoons lemon juice

175ml (6fl oz) mild olive oil

¼–½ teaspoon wholegrain mustard

a small bunch of dill, finely chopped

salt and freshly ground black pepper

---

1 Process the trout, crème fraîche, egg white, lemon rind, Tabasco sauce and a pinch of salt in a food processor until smooth. Transfer to a bowl, cover and chill for at least 30 minutes.

2 With wet hands, form the fish mixture into balls the size of a small walnut. Cover and chill again, if liked.

3 To make the dip, put all the ingredients in a screw-top jar and shake well together. Just before serving, shake again and pour into individual small bowls.

4 To serve, remove the trout balls from the refrigerator about 20 minutes before the meal is due to start. Pour enough stock to two-thirds fill a fondue pot into a saucepan and bring to the boil on the hob. Pour the stock into the warmed fondue pot, put over a burner and reheat until simmering. Poach a few balls at a time, until they rise to the surface. Keep more stock warm on the hob. Use a slotted spoon or Chinese wire strainer to transfer the fish balls to plates. Serve with the Mustard and Dill Dip.

Salmon Fondue with Chive Sauce and Cucumber

*T*HIS is a novel way of enjoying salmon. The chive sauce is lighter and healthier than traditional hollandaise sauce – which is likely to separate if it is kept waiting. Ideally, use salmon bones, skin and trimmings to make the stock.

SERVES 4–6

fish stock (see page 31), for cooking

about 500g (1¼lb) salmon fillet, cut into small bite-sized pieces

CUCUMBER

1 cucumber, peeled

3 tablespoons white wine vinegar

1½ teaspoons finely chopped dill

1½ teaspoons caster sugar

salt and freshly ground white or black pepper

CHIVE SAUCE

300ml (½ pint) half-fat crème fraîche

finely grated rind and juice of 1 small lemon

3½ tablespoons chopped chives

salt and freshly ground black pepper

1 Halve the cucumber lengthways and scoop out the seeds. Thinly slice the cucumber and mix with the other cucumber ingredients. Cover and leave in a cool place to marinate.

2 To make the chive sauce, stir all the ingredients together.

3 Just before serving, bring enough fish stock to two-thirds fill a fondue pot to the boil in a saucepan on the hob. Pour into the warmed fondue pot and put over a burner. Heat to simmering point. Poach the salmon until cooked to taste. Keep more stock warm on the hob.

4 Remove the salmon with a Chinese wire strainer or slotted spoon. Serve the salmon with the cucumber and the Chive Sauce.

Dashi Fondue with Prawn Wontons

DASHI is the basic stock used in Japanese cooking. It is made from dried bonito (a fish), nori seaweed and soy sauce, and can be bought in oriental foodshops. Frozen raw tiger prawns have greenish shells and are available from the wet fish counters of some supermarkets and good fishmongers. Most of the sauces, dips and salads in the book are suitable for serving with these wontons.

SERVES 4–6

24-30 wontons
flour, for dusting

2 × 10g (¹⁄₄oz) sachets of dashi

PRAWN FILLING

450g (1lb) large raw prawns, preferably tiger prawns, in their shells

2.5cm (1 inch) piece of ginger, very finely chopped

1 shallot, very finely chopped

1 tablespoon finely chopped coriander leaves

1 tablespoon sake or dry sherry

1 tablespoon soy sauce

1 egg white, lightly beaten

freshly ground black pepper

1 To make the filling, peel the prawns then, using a small sharp knife, cut a slit along the back of each prawn and remove the dark intestinal thread. Rinse the prawns and pat dry with paper towels. Chop finely.

2 Mix the prawns, ginger, shallot and coriander together in a bowl and mix in the sake or sherry, soy sauce, egg white and pepper. Cover and chill, if liked.

3 Spread out a wonton wrapper on a lightly floured surface and moisten the edges with water. Put a heaped teaspoon of the prawn mixture in the middle of the wrapper. Fold up two opposite corners to meet in the centre and pinch at the top to seal. Repeat with the other two corners, pinching along the edges as well as at the top. Cover and chill for up to 4 hours, if liked. Return to room temperature 30 minutes before the meal is due to start.

4 To serve, make up the dashi according to the packet instructions and bring to the boil in a saucepan on the hob. Pour enough dashi stock into a warmed fondue pot to two-thirds fill it, and put over a burner. Reheat until simmering.

5 Poach the wontons in batches in the stock for about 2–3 minutes. They will sink to the bottom at first, then rise to the surface; nudge free any that stick to the bottom. Keep more dashi warm on the hob. Remove the wontons with a Chinese wire strainer or slotted spoon.

Leek Fondue with Choux Cheese Dippers

*T*HE Choux Cheese Dippers can be made a day in advance, kept in an airtight container overnight then refreshed in a low–moderate oven for 5–10 minutes. Or they can be made longer ahead, frozen until just before required and refreshed from frozen for 20 minutes in a low–moderate oven.

SERVES 4–6

50g (2oz) unsalted butter

900g (2lb) leeks, thinly sliced into rings

about 150ml (5fl oz) vegetable or chicken stock (see pages 32 and 33)

freshly grated nutmeg

salt and freshly ground black pepper

CHOUX CHEESE DIPPERS

25g (1oz) unsalted butter, diced

35g (1¼oz) self-raising flour

1 large egg, beaten

2 tablespoons freshly grated Parmesan cheese, plus extra for sprinkling

¾ tablespoon chopped parsley or a pinch each of mustard powder and cayenne pepper

salt and freshly ground black pepper

1 To make the choux cheese dippers, preheat the oven to 200°C/400°F/Gas Mark 6. Gently heat the butter with 4½ tablespoons water in a small saucepan until the butter has just melted, then increase the heat and bring quickly to the boil. Immediately draw the pan from the heat and add all the flour. Beat well with a wooden spoon or electric whisk until smooth. Gradually beat or whisk in the egg, beating or whisking well after each addition. Add the cheese, parsley or mustard powder and cayenne pepper and seasoning towards the end.

2 Spoon the mixture into 1cm (½ inch) rounds on a non-stick baking sheet. Sprinkle a little Parmesan cheese over the tops and bake for 12–15 minutes, or until puffed and golden. Transfer to a wire rack to cool.

3 To make the fondue, heat the butter in a large frying pan or saucepan, add the leeks and cook for a couple of minutes or so, then cover the pan and cook gently, shaking the pan occasionally, until the leeks are very tender.

4 Leave to cool slightly then tip into a blender or food processor and purée to the desired coarseness.

5 To serve, return to the rinsed pan and add enough stock to give the right consistency. Season with nutmeg, salt and pepper and heat through. Pour the leek purée into a warmed fondue pot – it should be half to three-quarters full – and put over a burner until very hot. Spear the Choux Cheese Dippers on to fondue forks and scoop them through the purée.

Fondue with Butternut Squash Gnocchi

GNOCCHI are light little Italian 'dumplings'. I have specified butternut or kabocha squash (both of which can be bought from good supermarkets in the autumn) because they have the best flavour and a firm, dry texture. The sauce can be made 4–5 days in advance and kept covered in the refrigerator.

SERVES 4–6

350g (12oz) butternut or kabocha squash, cut into 2.5cm (1 inch) cubes

225g (½lb) potatoes, cut into 2.5cm (1 inch) cubes

1 egg yolk

115g (4oz) plain flour, plus extra for dusting

vegetable stock (see page 32), for cooking

salt and freshly ground black pepper

freshly grated mature pecorino or Parmesan cheese, to serve

BASIL AND MUSTARD SAUCE

2 egg yolks

1 tablespoon Dijon mustard

2 tablespoons finely chopped basil

25g (1oz) capers

3 tablespoons lemon juice

450ml (16fl oz) olive oil

freshly ground black pepper

1 Steam the squash and potatoes in a covered steaming basket over simmering water for 10–12 minutes until tender. Push through a mouli-légumes (vegetable mill) or a ricer into a clean saucepan, or mash with a potato masher. Put over a low heat for 1 minute or so to dry out.

2 Tip the vegetables into a large bowl and beat in the egg yolk, flour and seasoning. Leave to cool.

3 To make the sauce, put the egg yolks, mustard, basil, capers and lemon juice in a blender or food processor. Process to mix together. With the motor running, slowly pour in the oil in a thin, steady stream until the sauce has the consistency of whipped cream. Season with pepper and transfer to serving bowls.

4 To serve, put enough stock to two-thirds fill a fondue pot in a saucepan on the hob and bring to a rolling boil. Carefully pour into the warmed fondue pot over a burner and return to the boil. Drop teaspoonfuls of the squash and potato mixture into the stock. Once the liquid returns to the boil, simmer the gnocchi in batches for about 1½ minutes until they have risen to the surface and are softening slightly around the edges.

5 Use a slotted spoon or Chinese wire strainer to transfer the gnocchi to plates and sprinkle with Pecorino or Parmesan cheese. Serve with the Basil and Mustard Sauce.

Fondue with Salmon and Prawn Balls

I have served these both as the first course for an informal dinner party, and as the main course of a light summer lunch for fewer friends. Serve with Mayonnaise or Extra Light Mayonnaise (see page 105).

SERVES 4–6

350g (12oz) skinned salmon fillet

115g (4oz) peeled prawns

2 large egg whites

1 teaspoon baking powder

15g (½oz) cornflour

finely grated rind of 1 orange

1 teaspoon bottled green peppercorns, drained and rinsed

salt and freshly ground black pepper

fish stock (see page 31), for cooking

---

1 Put the salmon, prawns, egg whites, baking powder and cornflour into a food processor and process until the mixture is smooth.

2 Transfer the mixture to a bowl and stir in the orange rind, peppercorns and seasoning. Cover and chill for at least 30 minutes.

3 With wet hands, form the mixture into small balls. Cover and chill again, if liked. Return to room temperature 20 minutes before serving.

4 To serve, pour enough stock to two-thirds fill a fondue pot into a saucepan and bring to the boil on the hob. Pour the stock into the warmed fondue pot, put over a burner and reheat until simmering. Poach a few fish balls at a time until they rise to the surface. Keep more stock warm on the hob. Use a slotted spoon or Chinese wire strainer to transfer the balls to plates.

Tomato and Red Pepper Fondue

*T*HIS fondue looks beautifully sunny and warming, and tastes richly appetising, quite belying the fact that it is healthy. Dippers can include bread, cheese, vegetables, prawns, pieces of cooked sausage or cured sausages such as salami etc., and small rolls of ham.

SERVES 6

4 large red peppers	1 bay leaf
900g (2lb) well-flavoured tomatoes	1 sprig of rosemary
2 tablespoons virgin olive oil	about 5 sprigs of thyme
1 large onion, chopped	vegetable stock (see page 32)
1 leek, chopped	salt and freshly ground black pepper
4 cloves garlic, crushed	

1 Preheat the grill. Grill the peppers and tomatoes until the skins are charred and blistered and the flesh has softened.

2 Meanwhile, heat the oil in a saucepan. Add the onion, leek, garlic and herbs, cover and cook gently until the vegetables are soft. Discard the herbs.

3 Peel the peppers and tomatoes, leaving some of the charred skin on, if liked, to give an extra smoky flavour to the fondue. Remove the seeds (keep the tomato seeds for casseroles, soups and stocks).

4 Put all the vegetables in a blender, add a little of the stock and mix until smooth.

5 Return to the rinsed pan and add enough stock to give the right consistency for a fondue. Season to taste.

6 To serve, heat the fondue until it is bubbling.

Beef in Mushroom Broth Fondue

*T*HIS special fondue has a wonderfully rich-flavoured stock that leaves you with a delicious soup.

─────────── SERVES 6–8 ───────────

900g (2lb) fillet of beef, thinly sliced
   diagonally

POACHING LIQUOR

225g (½lb) leeks, left whole

2 carrots, left whole

2 small turnips, left whole

1 small onion studded with 2 cloves

¼ head celery, halved lengthways

225g (½lb) tomatoes, quartered

1 bay leaf, partially torn

a small handful of chervil

2 sprigs of thyme

½ small head of garlic, halved lengthways

1.5 litres (2½ pints) chicken stock (see
   page 33)

25g (1oz) dried ceps

freshly ground black pepper

─────────── TO SERVE ───────────

Rémoulade Sauce (see page 109)
breads (see pages 127–137)
cornichons

VEGETABLES
For example:

12 baby carrots

12 baby leeks

12 baby turnips

12 small new potatoes

4 small bundles of French beans

1 At least 3 hours before the meal, put all the ingredients for the poaching liquid, except the ceps, into a large saucepan and simmer very gently for 2 hours.

2 Meanwhile, soak the ceps in hot water for 30 minutes. Remove with a slotted spoon and squeeze the liquid from the ceps back into the soaking liquid. Strain the soaking liquid through muslin or a clean tea-towel, into the simmering stock. Add the ceps to the stock as well.

3 Bring a large saucepan of salted water to the boil. Cook each type of vegetable separately until just tender. Drain, refresh under running cold water, then drain again.

4 To serve the fondue, bring the stock to the boil in a saucepan on the hob. Two-thirds fill a warmed fondue pot with the stock and put over a burner. Reheat until simmering. Guests use fondue forks, chopsticks or long wooden skewers to dip the meat into the stock then transfer it to plates to eat with the Rémoulade Sauce and cornichons. Then a few of the vegetables are added to the stock as required, and heated through for 1–2 minutes. Any remaining stock can be eaten as soup, accompanied by bread.

Mongolian Hotpot

LAMB is the traditional meat for a Mongolian hotpot because it is the predominant meat of the region, and authentically the stock should be made from lamb bones and trimmings, but it has a rather distinctive flavour that is not to everyone's liking. Fish do not feature since they are not part of the local diet. Small sesame buns are a traditional accompaniment; they can be bought in some Asian food shops.

SERVES 6

900g (2lb) lean lamb, cut diagonally into thin slices or strips

2 packs of fresh bean curd, cut into bite-sized cubes

lamb, veal or vegetable stock (see pages 33 and 32), for cooking

Arrange the lamb in a single layer on individual plates. Arrange the bean curd in a separate bowl. Cover all the items with cling film and leave in a cool place until required.

VEGETABLES
a selection of:

Chinese leaves, shredded

spinach, washed, patted dry and shredded

oyster mushrooms, thinly sliced

broccoli florets

Prepare as necessary, and arrange in small bowls or on plates. Cover with cling film and keep cool.

NOODLES

225g (½lb) cellophane noodles

Pour boiling water over the noodles and leave for 10–15 minutes until softened. Drain and put into a bowl. Cover with cling film and leave in a cool place until required.

MASTER SAUCE

1 fresh red chilli, seeded and finely
   chopped

4 tablespoons finely chopped spring
   onions, white and green parts

3 tablespoons soy sauce

1 tablespoon sesame oil

Stir all the ingredients together, adjusting the levels to taste.

———————————————— To Serve ————————————————

sesame buns (optional)

soy sauce

fish sauce

shrimp paste

sesame oil

chilli oil

sesame paste

caster sugar

finely chopped garlic

chopped chives

chopped coriander

red vinegar

finely chopped spring onions, white and
   green parts

Reheat the sesame buns, if serving, and place around the pot. Put the remaining items in individual bowls, and put them around the pot.

To serve the hotpot, either heat the stock in the hotpot until simmering, or bring enough to two-thirds fill a fondue pot to the boil in a saucepan on the hob, then pour it into the warmed fondue pot, put over a burner and reheat until simmering. Guests are armed with a plate, chopsticks and/or a fondue fork, a soup spoon, and a small bowl (for the sauce), and help themselves to spoonfuls of the sauce, and other additional flavourings. Using chopsticks or a fondue fork, they lift up pieces of meat and dip them in the simmering stock and then into the sauce. When they have eaten all the meat they want, add the vegetables to the pot, as required, for just as long as it takes to soften them slightly; add the bean curd for as long as needed to heat it through. Like the meat, these are dipped into the sauce before being eaten. When all the vegetables and bean curd are finished, warm the noodles either in the pot or in a separate bowl of boiling water, then transfer them to the individual bowls. When the noodles have been eaten, divide the stock among the bowls. Guests mix it with the remaining sauce in the bowls, and drink it as a soup.

Chrysanthemum Hotpot

*T*HIS hotpot contains chicken, beef and seafood, and gets its name from the chrysanthemum petals that are floated on the cooking liquid.

SERVES 6

350g (12oz) chicken breasts, cut diagonally across the grain into very thin strips or slices

225g (½lb) rump or fillet steak, cut diagonally across the grain into thin slices or strips

350g (12oz) firm white fish such as cod, haddock or monkfish, thinly sliced across the grain

24 raw prawns, unpeeled

16 raw clams (optional)

chicken or vegetable stock (see pages 33 and 32), for cooking

chrysanthemum flower

Arrange the chicken, beef and fish in single layers on separate plates. Peel the pawns then, using the tip of a small sharp knife, slit along the back of each prawn, cutting almost but not quite all the way through. Remove and discard the dark intestinal thread. Arrange the prawns on a plate. Rinse the clams well, if using, and put in a bowl. Scatter the curled spring onions (see Vegetables, below) over each plate, then cover each plate with cling film and leave in a cool place.

VEGETABLES

8 spring onions, white and green parts, cut into 5cm (2 inch) lengths

a selection of:

spinach, rinsed, patted dry and shredded

oyster mushrooms, thinly sliced

mangetout

courgettes, cut into thin strips

baby carrots, cut into thin strips

1 Split the ends of each length of spring onion, and drop into cold water. Leave until the ends curl, then drain well and pat dry.

2 Put the other vegetables in separate bowls. Cover with cling film and leave in a cool place.

NOODLES

175g (6oz) cellophane noodles

Pour boiling water over the noodles and leave for 10–15 minutes until softened. Drain and put into a bowl. Cover the noodles with cling film and leave in a cool place until required.

─────────────────── FOR DIPPING ───────────────────

6 eggs	sesame oil
light and dark soy sauces	finely chopped chilli
caster sugar	grated fresh ginger
rice vinegar	finely chopped spring onions

To serve the hotpot, either heat the stock in the hotpot until simmering, or bring enough to two-thirds fill a fondue pot to the boil in a saucepan on the hob, pour it into the warmed fondue pot, put over a burner and reheat until simmering.

Uncover the bowls and plates and put them around the hotpot or fondue. Separate the chysanthemum flower into petals and place them in a bowl.

Guests break an egg into their dipping bowls, then add about 1 tablespoon soy sauce, a small pinch of sugar, a dash of rice vinegar and other flavourings, to taste, and lightly beat all the ingredients together.

Using chopsticks or a fondue fork, each person dips a piece of chicken, beef, fish, prawns, or clams if using, in the simmering stock. As soon as it is cooked, it is dipped in the egg-soy mixture, then eaten. When the chicken, beef, fish and shellfish have been eaten, the vegetables are added to the pot as required, and cooked long enough to tenderise them, then dipped in the sauce. When they are finished, warm the noodles, either in the pot or in a separate bowl of boiling water, then transfer them to the individual bowls. When the noodles have been eaten, divide the stock among the bowls, mix it with the remaining sauce, and drink as a soup with the chrysanthemum petals floating on the surface.

Singapore Steamboat

*I*NSTEAD of using prawns for the balls you could use white fish, or make half of them from fish and half from prawns. You could also serve some uncooked prawns and scallops or queen scallops. 1½ tablespoons of grated ginger can be substituted for the chilli in the vinegar.

SERVES 6

175g (6oz) fillet of beef (can be taken from the less expensive tail end), well chilled

175g (6oz) pork fillet (tenderloin), well chilled

175g (6oz) lamb fillet, well chilled

175g (6oz) chicken breast, well chilled

Using a very sharp knife, slice the meats and chicken into the thinnest possible slices. Arrange each meat on a separate plate. Cover with cling film and refrigerate.

PRAWN BALLS

350g (12oz) raw, peeled prawns

1½–2½ teaspoons cornflour

1 plump or 2 small spring onions, finely chopped

¾ teaspoon finely grated orange rind, if making fish balls

1 small egg white, lightly beaten

Put the prawns and 1½ teaspoons cornflour into a food processor or blender and mix until smooth. Mix in the spring onion(s), and orange rind if making fish balls. Stir in the egg white and more cornflour if necessary to bind the mixture, which should be firm enough to handle. Moisten your hands and roll the mixture into walnut-sized balls. Put on a plate, cover with cling film and refrigerate until required.

VEGETABLES

A selection of:

mangetout

French beans

baby sweetcorn

oyster mushrooms

shiitake mushrooms

asparagus spears

Prepare the vegetables as necessary and cut into bite-sized pieces.

Arrange in small bowls or on plates, cover with cling film and keep in a cool place until required.

NOODLES

350g (12oz) thin rice noodles

Cook the noodles according to the instructions on the packet. Drain, refresh in running cold water, drain again, then cover with cling film and set aside until required.

CHILLI VINEGAR

3 tablespoons rice vinegar

1½ tablespoons water

2 teaspoons sugar

½–1 red chilli, seeded and finely sliced

Mix all the ingredients together in a small bowl.

COCONUT SAUCE

2 teaspoons groundnut oil

1 small onion, finely chopped

5cm (2 inch) piece from the thick end of a lemon grass stalk, bruised and thinly sliced

¾ teaspoon crushed coriander seeds

75g (3oz) piece of coconut cream

about 3 tablespoons stock

Heat the oil in a frying pan or saucepan, add the onion, lemon grass and coriander seeds and fry until the onion has softened. Stir in the coconut cream. When it has melted, add enough stock to make a dipping sauce.

DIPPING SAUCE

2 tablespoons tomato purée

2 tablespoons water

1 teaspoon soy sauce

1 teaspoon toasted sesame oil

1 red chilli, seeded and finely chopped

Mix all the ingredients together.

STOCK

1 litre (1¾ pints) chicken or vegetable stock (see pages 33 and 32)

1½ tablespoons chopped coriander

5cm (2 inch) piece from the thick end of a lemon grass stalk, thinly sliced

2 spring onions, thinly sliced

To serve, bring the stock ingredients to the boil in a saucepan on the hob. Two-thirds fill a warmed fondue pot with the stock and put over a burner. Reheat until simmering. Guests use fondue forks, chopsticks, long wooden skewers or a Chinese wire strainer to dip the meat and fish and then the vegetables into the stock, to eat with the sauces and Chilli Vinegar.

When all the meat, fish and vegetables have been eaten, warm the noodles, either in the pot or in a separate bowl of boiling water, then transfer them to the individual bowls. Ladle the remaining stock, which will have become concentrated, into the bowls.

Simple Steamboat

*T*HE stock for this simplified version of the oriental hotpot theme is made from convenience foods. By the time the meats have been cooked there is a tasty soup to finish off with. More or less any of the dips, sauces and salads in the book can be served with this fondue. It is a good idea to include some good bread.

——————————————————— SERVES 6 ———————————————————

1 chicken stock cube

570ml (1 pint) fresh concentrated chicken stock (available in cartons)

40g (1½oz) dried wild mushrooms

250g (9oz) fillet or rump steak, cut diagonally across the grain into strips or cubes

250g (9oz) pork fillet, cut diagonally across the grain into slim strips

250g (9oz) leg of lamb, cut diagonally across the grain into strips or cubes

250g (9oz) chicken breasts, cut diagonally across the grain into slim strips

about 3 tablespoons dry sherry

1 Bring 570ml (1 pint) water to the boil in a saucepan. Add the stock cube and stir to dissolve. Add the stock and dried mushrooms and simmer gently for 30 minutes.

2 Two-thirds fill a warmed fondue pot with the prepared stock, put over a burner and reheat until simmering. People now start dipping the meat and chicken pieces.

3 When everyone has finished, pour the sherry into the stock left in the fondue pot and serve as a soup.

Oil Fondues

Oil fondues cook food quickly, so it should be cut into suitably sized pieces or pre-cooked.

It is preferable to use good-quality, tender cuts of meat (although slightly tougher ones can be marinated to tenderise them), and free-range chicken from a reputable supplier. Prepare meat, poultry and fish shortly before the meal: if the cut pieces of meat are left for too long the juices may run out and make the meat dry when cooked. (If it is too *wet* when lowered into the hot fat, it will splutter dangerously.) To make slicing easier, chill the meat in the freezer for about an hour or until partially frozen. Use a sharp knife with a flexible blade and cut diagonally across the grain. Pork and chicken should be cut into very thin slices to ensure they are cooked right through. Beef and lamb can be cut into slightly thicker slices, or cubes or strips, because thorough cooking is not so important – indeed, many people like them to still be pink in the centre. Lay out the slices in a single layer or they will stick together.

Cut vegetables to the required size and keep, covered with cling film, in a cool place until required.

Cooking in hot oil is a fierce method of cooking, so most foods, especially delicate or tender ones like fish, need to be coated in some way – with a batter or breadcrumbs, for example – to keep them moist and succulent.

To serve an oil fondue, measure the amount of oil you will need to half-fill your fondue pot and heat it to the required temperature, always in the range of 180–190°C/350–375°F, in a saucepan on the hob. (To test the temperature without a thermometer, drop in a cube of bread: when the oil is at the correct temperature it will sizzle in about 40 seconds.) To prevent the hot oil cooling down too much when transferred to the fondue pot, fill the pot with boiling water, to warm it. Pour out the water and dry the pot thoroughly. Carefully pour in enough hot oil to half-fill the pot. It is important not to over-fill it as the oil may froth up and spill over when cold food is added. You can add more oil as the evening progresses; preheat any that you add to avoid unduly cooling the oil in the pot.

Only a few pieces of food should be cooked at a time to avoid overcrowding the pot and cooling the oil; if the oil is not hot enough, the food will become soggy rather than be crisp and dry. It is a good idea to check the temperature of the oil in the fondue pot during cooking – it will be lowered every time food is added and may not fully recover if a lot is added in quick succession.

Fondue Bourguignonne (see page 77) is probably the first oil-cooked fondue that springs to mind; then there is Japanese tempura.

Tempura was introduced into Japan by Portuguese missionaries as a way to cook fish, but now it is often a combination of meat, fish, shellfish, vegetables and bean curd, served with a selection of dips and sauces. Feel free to include whatever combinations of ingredients you fancy when making a tempura.

Tempura batter is characterised by being especially light: it is made from an ice-cold liquid, either water or lager, which is mixed briefly (a few lumps don't matter) with flour. And unlike other batters, which are usually left to stand, it is made immediately before it is to be used. A whisked egg white is sometimes folded in just before the batter is used. Traditionally, rice flour is used, which helps with the lightness: you can use rice flour or cornflour, a mixture of cornflour and ordinary plain flour, or plain flour.

The batter cooks very quickly so the food inside must also be quick-cooking. Once cooked, the fritters should not be covered as they will lose their crispness. In the recipes that follow I have specified olive oil where the flavour is appropriate.

To cook and serve tempura, each guest picks up a piece of their chosen food with chopsticks, dips it in the batter, allows any excess batter to flow off, then lowers the food carefully into the oil. The pieces should be added a few at a time so that the temperature of the oil is maintained. When the batter is lightly browned, the food is removed from the pan, again using chop-sticks, and drained on paper towels before being dipped into the accompanying sauces and dips. So line a serving plate or basket with paper towels. I provide a Chinese wire strainer, or a slotted spoon, to assist with scooping the cooked food from the oil as the food could be overcooked while someone who is not adept at wielding chopsticks frantically tries to fish out their quickly-darkening morsel.

Vegetable Tempura

MANY different vegetables can be used. For quick cooking they need to be cut into small pieces; vegetables like cauliflower florets are best if par-boiled then left until cold.

SERVES 4

---

1 red onion, thinly sliced

175g (6oz) shiitake mushrooms, sliced

115g (4oz) mangetout, trimmed

115g (4oz) small broccoli florets

1 sweet potato, thinly sliced

4–8 spring onions, cut into 7.5cm (3 inch) lengths

oil for cooking

LAGER BATTER

150g (5oz) rice flour or mixed cornflour and plain flour

1 large egg, separated

225ml (8fl oz) ice-cold lager or water

DIPPING SAUCE

4cm (1½ inch) piece of ginger, grated
6 tablespoons soy sauce

4 tablespoons mirin or dry sherry

---

1 To make the dipping sauce, mix all the ingredients together and divide among four small bowls.

2 Make the batter just before serving. Put all the ingredients except the egg white into a bowl and whisk very briefly; do not overmix – the batter should be lumpy. Whisk the egg white until stiff, then carefully fold into the batter until just evenly blended.

3 To serve, pour enough oil to half-fill a fondue pot into a saucepan on the hob and heat to 190°C/375°F. Carefully pour the oil into the warmed fondue pot, put over a burner and reheat.

4 Dip three or four pieces of vegetable at a time into the batter, allow excess batter to flow off, then cook until crisp and golden underneath. Turn the pieces over and cook on the other side. Using a slotted spoon or Chinese wire strainer, transfer the fritters to paper towels to drain briefly. Serve with the dipping sauce.

Fondue of Oriental Mushroom Fritters with Curried Peanut Sauce

A light crisp batter encloses succulent spiced cooked mushrooms, served with a satay-style sauce.

SERVES 4

4–5 tablespoons oil, plus oil for cooking
450g (1lb) button mushrooms
a pinch of dried chilli flakes
2 teaspoons Chinese five-spice powder
65g (2½oz) cornflour

65g (2½oz) self-raising flour
½ teaspoon baking powder
1 egg white
salt and freshly ground black pepper

CURRIED PEANUT SAUCE

2½ tablespoons crunchy peanut butter
½ clove garlic, finely crushed and
    chopped
½–1 teaspoon soy sauce
½ teaspoon curry powder

½ teaspoon clear honey
150ml (5fl oz) vegetable or chicken stock
a little lime or lemon juice, to taste

1 Heat 1–2 tablespoons oil in a frying pan, add the mushrooms and cook for 2 minutes, or until beginning to soften. Sprinkle over the chilli flakes and five-spice powder and stir in. Transfer to a sieve over a bowl and leave to cool.

2 To make the sauce, put the peanut butter, garlic, soy sauce, curry powder and honey into a small saucepan and stir together. Pour in the stock, stirring, then bring to the boil. Lower the heat and simmer for 3–4 minutes. Add a little lime or lemon juice.

3 Sift the cornflour, flour, baking powder and seasoning into a bowl. Make up the juices that have drained from the mushrooms to 150ml (5fl oz) with ice-cold water and gradually add to the cornflour mixture with 3 tablespoons oil, stirring to make a smooth batter.

4 Whisk the egg white until stiff, then carefully fold into the batter until just evenly blended.

5 Pour enough oil to half-fill a fondue pot into a saucepan on the hob and heat to 190°C/375°F. Carefully pour the oil into the warmed fondue pot, put over a burner and reheat. Cook a few mushrooms at a time until crisp and golden. Using a slotted spoon or Chinese wire strainer, transfer the mushrooms to paper towels to drain briefly. Serve with the Curried Peanut Sauce.

Fennel Fritters Fondue

*F*INE polenta, which is sometimes sold under the name of corn-meal, gives a delicious crunchy texture to these fritters.

SERVES 4–6

3 fennel bulbs	2 eggs, beaten
about 150g (5oz) fine polenta (cornmeal)	olive oil for cooking
3 tablespoons freshly grated Parmesan	freshly ground black pepper

1 Cut the fennel bulbs lengthways into slices no thicker than 1cm (½ inch). Place in a single layer in a steaming basket, cover and steam over boiling water until just tender. Leave to cool.

2 Mix together the fine polenta, Parmesan cheese and pepper.

3 Dip the fennel slices in the beaten eggs, allowing the excess to flow off. Toss the slices in the polenta mixture. Spread out on a large tray, cover and leave in a cool place until required.

4 Pour enough oil to half-fill a fondue pot into a saucepan on the hob and heat to 190°C/375°F. Carefully pour into the warmed fondue pot, put over a burner and reheat. Cook a few fennel slices at a time until crisp and golden. Using a slotted spoon or Chinese wire strainer, transfer the fritters to paper towels to drain.

Golden Thai Vegetable Balls

❧

SERVE these light, melt-in-the-mouth balls with any of the dipping sauces on pages 101–113.

SERVES 4–6

350g (12oz) courgettes, grated

225g (½lb) cauliflower, grated

225g (½lb) carrots, grated

50g (2oz) peanuts, finely chopped

1 stalk of lemon grass, crushed and very finely chopped

1 fresh red chilli, seeded and very finely chopped

4cm (1½ inch) piece of ginger, finely grated

115g (4oz) fresh breadcrumbs

1 whole egg, plus 1 egg white

rice flour, or cornflour, and sesame seeds, for coating

salt

oil for cooking

1 Put the vegetables, peanuts, lemon grass, chilli, ginger, salt and breadcrumbs into a bowl and stir together. Add the egg and egg white and mix well until bound together. Cover and chill for at least 30 minutes.

2 Form the mixture into small balls, squeezing them together.

3 Mix some rice flour or cornflour and sesame seeds together on a plate or in a shallow dish and roll the balls in the mixture to coat evenly, pressing the coating in.

4 Cover and chill again. Remove the balls from the refrigerator about 20 minutes before the meal is due to be served.

5 Pour enough oil to half-fill a fondue pot into a saucepan on the hob and heat to 190°C/375°F. Carefully pour the oil into the warmed fondue pot, put over a burner and reheat. Cook a few balls at a time until crisp and golden. Using a slotted spoon or Chinese wire strainer, transfer the balls to paper towels to drain briefly.

Cauliflower Fritters

*T*HE Parmesan cheese adds a more-ish flavour to the batter and melts into it without going stringy. Chopped basil, parsley or thyme, a pinch of mustard powder or a little curry powder can be added to the batter. Most of the dips, sauces and salads in the book are suitable accompaniments.

SERVES 4–6

450g (1lb) cauliflower florets	1 egg, beaten
40g (1½oz) plain flour	oil for cooking
25g (1oz) freshly grated Parmesan cheese	freshly ground black pepper

1 Spread the cauliflower florets in a single layer in a steaming basket and steam until tender. Cut each floret lengthways in half. Leave to cool.

2 Mix together the flour, Parmesan cheese and pepper. Slowly pour in 8 tablespoons water and the egg, stirring to make a smooth batter. Leave to stand for at least 30 minutes.

3 Pour enough oil to half-fill a fondue pot into a saucepan on the hob and heat to 190°C/375°F. Carefully pour the oil into the warmed fondue pot, put over a burner and reheat. Dip the cauliflower florets in the batter, allowing the excess to flow back into the bowl. Cook a few cauliflower sprigs at a time until crisp and golden. Using a slotted spoon or Chinese wire strainer, transfer the fritters to paper towels to drain briefly.

Fondue-Cooked Crisp-Coated Courgette Chips

◉

POLENTA gives an appetising, contrasting, crisp coating to the delicate thin courgette 'chips' inside. Mediterranean Dip (see page 111), Rémoulade (see page 109), Basil and Mustard Sauce (see page 46) and Sun-Dried Tomato Aïoli (see page 108) are just some of the suitable accompaniments.

SERVES 4–6

4 courgettes

about 6 tablespoons fine polenta (cornmeal)

1 teaspoon cayenne pepper

300ml (½ pint) milk

olive oil for cooking

salt

1 Cut the courgettes into slim chips.

2 Season the polenta with the cayenne pepper and salt.

3 Dip the courgette chips in the milk then coat evenly in the polenta mixture; shake off the excess.

4 Pour enough oil to half-fill a fondue pot into a saucepan on the hob and heat to 190°C/375°F. Carefully pour the oil into the warmed fondue pot, put over a burner and reheat to 180°C/350°F. Cook several courgette chips at a time until crisp and golden. Using a slotted spoon or Chinese wire strainer, transfer the chips to paper towels to drain briefly.

Roast Root Vegetable Beignets

*T*HE batter is a particularly full-flavoured one – not only is it made with lager, it also contains chopped basil or parsley, and capers. Accompany the beignets with a selection of sauces, salads and breads.

SERVES 4–6

450g (1lb) mixed root vegetables such as parsnips, carrots, celeriac and turnips, cut into wedges

225g (½lb) cooked beetroot, cut into wedges

1 tablespoon olive oil, plus olive oil for cooking

350g (12oz) self-raising flour

2 tablespoons chopped basil or parsley

25g (1oz) capers

300ml (½ pint) cold lager

1 egg white

coarse sea salt and freshly ground black pepper

1 Preheat the oven to 200°C/400°F/Gas Mark 6. Spread all the vegetables, including the beetroot, in a roasting tin, pour over the 1 tablespoon oil and stir the vegetables around so that they are coated in oil. Bake for 25–30 minutes until golden and tender. Transfer to a wire rack lined with paper towels to cool.

2 Put the flour, basil or parsley, capers, lager and pepper in a food processor. Process briefly until just evenly blended. Pour into a bowl.

3 Just before serving, whisk the egg white until stiff but not dry. Using a large metal spoon, carefully fold into the batter in batches.

4 Pour enough oil to half-fill a fondue pot into a saucepan on the hob and heat to 190°C/375°F. Carefully pour the oil into the warmed fondue pot, put over a burner and reheat. Dip the vegetables in the batter, allowing the excess to flow back into the bowl. Cook a few at a time until golden and crisp. Using a slotted spoon or Chinese wire strainer, transfer to paper towels to drain briefly. Sprinkle with coarse salt before eating.

Cheese Tempura

◉

I know this is an unorthodox recipe – cheese was until very recently almost unknown in Japan – but the classic crisp, light character of a tempura batter is just right for enclosing soft, just-melting cheese. Edam cheese can work well; I always try to keep any I buy for at least a month, preferably longer, to give it more time to mature and develop a stronger flavour. (If it is pre-packed or wrapped in plastic or cling film, re-wrap it in greaseproof paper and put it inside a plastic bag or overwrap it with foil.) Serve the tempura with your choice of dips and sauces.

--- SERVES 4 ---

350–450g (12–16oz) Fontina or other semi-soft cheese

65g (2½oz) cornflour, plus extra for dusting

1 egg

65g (2½oz) plain flour

175g (6fl oz) iced lager or water

olive oil for cooking

freshly ground black pepper

---

1 Remove the rind or crust from the cheese. Cut the cheese into cubes. Dust the cubes in cornflour so they are lightly and evenly coated. Cover and refrigerate until ready to serve.

2 Just before serving, lightly whisk the egg with a fork, then lightly whisk in the cornflour, flour, pepper and lager or water until almost smooth.

3 Pour enough oil to half-fill a fondue pot into a saucepan on the hob and heat to 190°C/375°F. Carefully pour the oil into the warmed fondue pot, put over a burner and reheat. Spear the coated cheese on to long-handled forks and dip into the batter. Allow the excess to flow off, then cook until puffy, soft and golden. Touch on to paper towels to drain.

Fondue-Cooked Camembert Croquettes

CRISP on the outside and melting inside, these little croquettes are always popular. Tomato Salad (see page 120) and Red and Yellow Pepper Relish (see page 114) are good accompaniments.

SERVES 4–6

1 Camembert, chopped

50g (2oz) softened unsalted butter

150g (5oz) fromage frais

50g (2oz) plain flour, sifted, plus extra for coating

2 egg yolks

2 eggs, beaten

50g (2oz) cream crackers, reduced to fine crumbs

oil for cooking

freshly ground black pepper

1 Put the Camembert into a heatproof bowl and mash with a fork. Mash in the butter, then the fromage frais. Beat in the flour and pepper.

2 Place the bowl over a saucepan of simmering water and beat the mixture for 4–5 minutes until smooth.

3 Remove the pan from the heat and beat in the egg yolks. Leave to cool, then put in the refrigerator for at least 2 hours to become firm.

4 Form tablespoons of the mixture into balls. Roll them in flour, then dip in the beaten egg. Finally, roll them in the cream-cracker crumbs, pressing the crumbs in well, until evenly and completely covered. Chill again.

5 Pour enough oil to half-fill a fondue pot into a saucepan on the hob and heat to 190°C/375°F. Carefully pour the oil into the warmed fondue pot, put over a burner and reheat. Cook a few croquettes at a time until crisp and golden. Using a slotted spoon or Chinese wire strainer, transfer the croquettes to paper towels to drain briefly.

Fondue-Fried Cheese Gnocchi

GNOCCHI are usually poached, but for this fondue version they are fried to make them deliciously different.

SERVES 6

570ml (1 pint) milk

1 onion, sliced

4 cloves garlic, halved

1 clove

bouquet garni of 1 bay leaf, several parsley stalks and sprigs of thyme

115g (4oz) fine polenta (cornmeal)

200g (7oz) mature Cheddar cheese, grated

2 tablespoons freshly grated Parmesan

2 tablespoons chopped basil or parsley

1 teaspoon Dijon mustard

salt (optional) and freshly ground black pepper

oil for cooking

1 Pour the milk into a saucepan, add the onion, garlic, clove and bouquet garni and bring to the boil. Cover the pan, remove from the heat and leave to infuse for 30 minutes. Strain the milk.

2 Return the milk to the saucepan and bring to the boil. Sprinkle the polenta over the top, stirring with a wooden spoon. Cook, still stirring, for 1 minute or until the mixture thickens.

3 Draw the pan off the heat and stir in the cheeses, basil or parsley and mustard. Season generously with pepper; salt may not be needed because of the saltiness of the cheeses.

4 Spread the mixture in a 1cm (½ inch) layer in a shallow baking dish, cool, then chill in the refrigerator for at least 30 minutes. Cut into cubes.

5 Pour enough oil to half-fill a fondue pot into a saucepan on the hob and heat to 190°C/375°F. Carefully pour the oil into the warmed fondue pot, put over a burner and reheat. Cook a few gnocchi at a time until golden brown. Using a Chinese wire strainer or slotted spoon, transfer the gnocchi to paper towels to drain briefly. Eat while warm.

Oriental-Style Trout Goujons

Ⓔ

*H*ERE I have given a recipe for an oriental-style marinade, but if you prefer a more Mediterranean flavour, use a good olive oil, lemon juice and chopped herbs, such as dill, fennel or basil. Serve with a selection of dips, sauces and salads.

SERVES 4

450g (1lb) trout fillets

cornflour, for coating

beaten egg, for coating

fine breadcrumbs, for coating

olive oil for cooking

lime wedges, to serve

MARINADE

1 clove garlic, crushed

1cm ($\frac{1}{2}$ inch) piece of ginger, grated

2 spring onions, finely chopped

$\frac{1}{2}$ teaspoon Chinese five-spice powder

2 tablespoons sake or dry sherry

2 tablespoons flavourless oil

1 tablespoon lime juice

1 tablespoon sesame oil

---

1 Mix together the marinade ingredients.

2 Cut the trout into strips, add to the marinade, stir to coat, then cover and leave at room temperature for 1–2 hours.

3 Lift the trout from the marinade and pat dry. Roll the strips in the cornflour, then in the beaten egg. Allow the excess egg to drain off before rolling the strips in breadcrumbs.

4 Pour enough oil to half-fill a fondue pot into a saucepan on the hob and heat to 190°C/375°F. Carefully pour the oil into a warmed fondue pot, put over a burner and reheat.

5 Spear the goujons on to long-handled forks and dip them into the hot oil until golden and crisp. Touch on to paper towels to drain briefly. Serve with lime wedges.

Shrimp Beignets

◉

BROWN shrimps, which are found mainly in shallow waters around Britain, are usually considered to have the sweetest flavour, so try to get some if you can. (If you have some potted in butter you will have to melt off the butter – which should have a good flavour – and use it for another purpose.) Otherwise, use pink shrimps. The beignets can be served with almost any of the dips and sauces and salads.

SERVES 4–6

130g (4½ oz) plain flour	oil for cooking
1 egg, separated	350g (12oz) peeled shrimps
about 150ml (5fl oz) lager, chilled	salt and cayenne pepper
1 tablespoon oil	lemon wedges, to serve

1 Sift the flour, salt and cayenne into a bowl. Make a well in the centre and gradually add the egg yolk and lager, mixing in the flour from the sides to make a smooth batter with the consistency of thick cream. Stir in the oil. Cover and leave for at least 30 minutes.

2 Pour enough oil to half-fill a fondue pot into a saucepan on the hob and heat to 190°C/375°F.

3 Meanwhile, whisk the egg white until stiff, then fold into the batter.

4 Carefully pour the oil into a warmed fondue pot, put over a burner and reheat.

5 Spear the shrimps on to long-handled forks and dip into the batter. Allow the excess to flow off, then cook the beignets in the hot oil until golden. Touch on to paper towels to drain briefly. Serve with lemon wedges.

Crispy Fish Fondue

*T*HIS is a very sociable and easy way of having one half of the ever-popular meal, fish and chips. Any filleted and skinned firm white fish can be used. It can be made more exotic by the accompaniments. Suitable dips and sauces include Sun-Dried Tomato Aïoli (see page 108), Oriental Tartare Sauce (see page 108), Grilled Red Pepper Sauce (see page 113), Oriental Mustard Sauce (see page 110) and Rémoulade Sauce (see page 109).

SERVES 4–6

700g (1½lb) cod, haddock or monkfish fillets, cut into bite-sized pieces

olive oil for cooking

lemon wedges, to serve

BATTER

115g (4oz) plain flour

2 tablespoons olive oil

2 egg whites

salt and freshly ground black pepper

1 To make the batter, sift the flour and seasoning into a bowl. Make a well in the centre and gradually pour in 150ml (5fl oz) water, mixing in the flour from the sides to make a smooth batter. Stir in the oil. Cover and leave for at least 30 minutes.

2 Just before serving, whisk the egg whites until stiff, then carefully fold them into the batter until just evenly blended.

3 Pour enough oil to half-fill a fondue pot into a saucepan on the hob and heat to 190°C/375°F. Carefully pour the oil into the warmed fondue pot, put over a burner and reheat. Dip several of the fish pieces at a time into the batter, then fry until crisp and golden. Transfer the fish to paper towels to drain briefly and serve with lemon wedges.

Oyster Tempura

ⓒ

PACIFIC oysters (which are farmed) are much cheaper than the expensive – and now quite scarce – native oysters. Pacific oysters can also be eaten all year round. Ask the fishmonger to open them for you if you would prefer not to do it yourself. Serve with a selection of dips and sauces.

SERVES 4–6

24 Pacific oysters, opened

3 cloves garlic, crushed and finely chopped

a few drops of Worcestershire sauce

a dash of Tabasco

$\frac{1}{2}$ teaspoon dried thyme

plain flour, for coating

olive oil for cooking

BATTER

2 eggs

225ml (8fl oz) iced water

a generous pinch of bicarbonate of soda

115g (4oz) plain flour

1 Dry the oysters. Mix together the garlic, Worcestershire sauce, Tabasco and thyme, and use to season the oysters. Toss the oysters in flour to coat them evenly. Shake off any excess flour.

2 To make the batter, whisk the eggs and water until frothy. Add the bicarbonate of soda and flour in one go and stir quickly a few times. Be careful not to overmix; there should be a few lumps – if you stir until the batter is smooth, you will end up with a heavy coating when it is fried.

3 Pour enough oil to half-fill a fondue pot into a saucepan on the hob and heat to 190°C/375°F. Carefully pour the oil into the warmed fondue pot, put over a burner and reheat. Dip a few oysters at a time in the batter and fry until crisp and golden. Transfer the oysters to paper towels to drain briefly.

Crab Cakes Fondue

𝒬

*T*HE crab cakes can be made well in advance and frozen until a few hours before they are required. Leave them to thaw in the refrigerator, then return them to room temperature about 30 minutes before cooking. Most of the accompaniments in the book can be served with the crab cakes.

SERVES 4–6

15g (½oz) unsalted butter

½ red pepper, finely chopped

1 celery stick, finely chopped

a bunch of spring onions, finely chopped

450g (1lb) fresh crabmeat

1 egg, beaten

1 tablespoon finely chopped parsley

1 tablespoon finely chopped basil

1 tablespoon Dijon mustard

about 200g (7oz) fresh breadcrumbs

salt and freshly ground black pepper

oil for cooking

1 Heat the butter in a small pan and fry the red pepper, celery and spring onions for about 5 minutes until softened. Transfer to a bowl and leave to cool.

2 Stir the crabmeat, egg, herbs, mustard and seasoning into the fried vegetables.

3 Form the mixture into small balls, then roll in the breadcrumbs to coat evenly; make sure the breadcrumbs are pressed in firmly. Leave in the refrigerator for at least 1 hour.

4 Pour enough oil to half-fill a fondue pot into a saucepan on the hob and heat to 190°C/375°F. Carefully pour the oil into the warmed fondue pot, put over a burner and reheat.

5 Fry the cakes in batches until crisp and brown. Drain briefly on paper towels.

Sesame-Coated Fish Balls with Spiced Ginger Sauce

○

SALMON, trout or prawns can be used in place of some of the white fish, and will give extra flavour and distinction to the fish balls.

───── SERVES 4 ─────

450g (1lb) white fish fillets

1 tablespoon finely chopped fresh ginger

3 spring onions, finely chopped

a pinch of dried chilli flakes

1 tablespoon chopped coriander

1 tablespoon soy sauce

1 tablespoon cornflour

2 eggs, beaten, plus beaten egg for coating

equal amounts of sesame seeds and breadcrumbs

salt and freshly ground black pepper

oil for cooking

SPICED GINGER SAUCE

$\frac{1}{4}$ teaspoon grated fresh ginger

$\frac{1}{4}$ teaspoon ground cumin

1 tablespoon tomato ketchup

5 tablespoons Mayonnaise (page 105)

1 Put the fish in a food processor and process until minced. Transfer to a bowl and stir in the ginger, spring onions, chilli flakes, coriander, soy sauce and cornflour.

2 Add the eggs to bind the mixture together. Season to taste. Cover and leave in the refrigerator for at least 1 hour.

3 To make the sauce, stir the ginger, cumin and tomato ketchup into the mayonnaise.

4 Shape the fish mixture into small balls. Dip them in beaten egg, then roll in a mixture of sesame seeds and breadcrumbs to coat evenly, pressing the coating in firmly. Return to the refrigerator.

5 Pour enough oil to half-fill a fondue pot into a saucepan on the hob and heat to 190°C/375°F. Carefully pour the oil into the warmed fondue pot, put over a burner and reheat. Cook a few fish balls at a time until crisp and brown. Remove and drain briefly on paper towels. Serve with the Spiced Ginger Sauce.

Fondue Bourguignonne

*F*ONDUE bourguignonne is the classy version of the French country dish *pot au feu*. Instead of one of the tougher cuts of meat being slowly cooked in a casserole, tender prime meat is quickly deep-fried in hot oil. Both dishes are served with similar accompaniments, such as gherkins, mustard, Rémoulade Sauce (see page 109), Horseradish sauce (see page 103 for a dipping version) or Mayonnaise (see page 105), but there is no reason why you should not serve it with accompaniments from other countries, such as Oriental Tartare Sauce (see page 108), Oriental Mustard Sauce (see page 110) or a dipping sauce. The Grilled Sweetcorn Salsa (see page 117) and Aubergine Relish (see page 115) are also good with the beef.

SERVES 4

about 700g (1½lb) rump or fillet steak   olive oil for cooking

1 Make the sauces or dips of your choice.

2 Shortly before the meal, use a sharp knife to remove any fat and sinews from the meat, then cut the meat across the grain into strips, thin slices or small cubes.

3 Pour enough oil to half-fill a fondue pot into a saucepan on the hob and heat to 190°C/375°F. Carefully pour the oil into a warmed fondue pot, put over a burner and reheat.

4 Lower a few pieces of meat at a time into the hot oil for 30–90 seconds, or until cooked to individual preference. Touch on to paper towels to drain, then transfer to an ordinary fork and eat with your chosen accompaniments.

Crispy Filo Prawns with Yogurt Chutney Dip

⊙

*I*T is not possible to say precisely how many sheets of filo pastry you will need because the sheets vary in size; to be on the safe side, have some spare ones handy. If the prawns are left to marinate in the refrigerator, transfer them to room temperature about 30 minutes before cooking.

SERVES 4–6

2.5cm (1 inch) piece of ginger, finely chopped or grated

3 cloves garlic, crushed and finely chopped

1 tablespoon soy sauce

1 tablespoon groundnut oil

1 tablespoon lime juice

500g (1¼lb) cooked large prawns, peeled and deveined

3–4 sheets of filo pastry

2 eggs, beaten, for brushing

oil for cooking

YOGURT CHUTNEY DIP

5 tablespoons double cream

5 tablespoons plain yogurt

2 tablespoons mango chutney

1 tablespoon chopped coriander

freshly ground black pepper

1 Mix together the ginger, garlic, soy sauce, oil and lime juice. Stir in the prawns so that they are coated with the marinade, cover and leave in a cool place for at least 2 hours, or overnight.

2 To make the dip, stir all the ingredients together.

3 Drain the prawns from the marinade and pat dry with paper towels.

4 Cut a sheet of filo pastry into approximately 7.5cm (3 inch) squares; keep the remaining sheets covered with a clean, damp tea-towel. Brush the edges of a square with beaten egg. Put a prawn in the centre and twist the filo over the prawn to make a neat bundle. Seal firmly. Repeat with the remaining filo and prawns.

5 Pour enough oil to half-fill a fondue pot into a saucepan on the hob and heat to 190°C/375°F. Carefully pour the oil into the warmed fondue pot, put over a burner and reheat.

6 Fry the prawns in batches until the pastry is crisp and brown. Serve with Yogurt Chutney Dip.

Bagna Cauda

BAGNA cauda is an oil-based garlicky-anchovy fondue from the Piedmonte region of Italy. There are quite a number of variations on the recipe: some use just oil and no butter, and the amounts and proportions of anchovies and garlic can vary, so feel free to make your own adjustments. Bagna cauda is traditionally eaten in spring, accompanied by cardoons and perhaps young artichoke hearts, but it can also be served with celery sticks, carrot sticks, fennel, chicory, courgettes, red peppers and plenty of bread.

SERVES 4

50g (2oz) unsalted butter, chopped

4 cloves garlic, crushed and very finely chopped

10 anchovy fillets

200ml (7fl oz) olive oil

freshly ground black pepper

1 Put the butter into a heavy fondue pot and heat until melted. Add the garlic and cook gently for a few minutes; do not allow to brown.

2 Add the anchovy fillets and mash them so that they disintegrate.

3 Very slowly stir in the oil, then cook gently, stirring most of the time, for about 10 minutes or until the mixture is smooth.

4 Season with plenty of pepper. The bagna cauda is now ready to be dipped into.

Chicken Liver and Bacon Bites Fondue

*T*HE amount of bacon you will need depends on the thickness of the rashers. Any sauce left after the end of the fondue can be kept in a screw-top jar in the refrigerator.

SERVES 4–6

about 350g (12oz) streaky bacon

225g (½lb) chicken livers
oil for cooking

AMERICAN SAUCE

1½ tablespoons oil

1 onion, finely chopped

2 cloves garlic, finely crushed

900g (2lb) tomatoes, peeled, seeded and chopped

3 tablespoons white wine vinegar

2 tablespoons Worcestershire sauce

1 teaspoon tomato purée

1 tablespoon curry powder

about 25g (1oz) sugar, to taste

salt and freshly ground black pepper

1 To make the sauce, heat the oil in a large frying pan, add the onion and fry until softened. Add the garlic towards the end.

2 Add the tomatoes, vinegar, Worcestershire sauce, tomato purée and curry powder and simmer, stirring occasionally, until the sauce has thickened; this will take about 30 minutes.

3 Stir in sugar and seasoning to taste. Set aside until required.

4 Remove the rinds from the bacon. Stretch each rasher with the back of a large knife, then cut across into halves.

5 Cut each chicken liver into two or three pieces. Wrap each piece in a length of bacon, and spear on to the end of a long skewer.

6 Pour enough oil to half-fill a fondue pot into a saucepan on the hob and heat to 190°C/375°F. Carefully pour into a warmed fondue pot, put over a burner and reheat. Cook the bites until

the bacon is golden and the liver is still pink in the centre.
Remove the bites and dip briefly on to paper towels to drain.
Serve with the American Sauce.

VARIATION
Water Chestnuts and Bacon Bites Fondue
Use water chestnuts instead of chicken livers.

Sweet Fondues

Sweet or dessert fondues are a comparatively recent idea from America, and a very convivial way to end a meal. Once, after a meal that had been very 'frosty', I abandoned the dessert I had planned to serve and instead quickly rustled up a wickedly delicious and slightly alcoholic fondue: the evening ended on a positively jolly note.

Chocolate fondues are the best known and most popular dessert fondues. Other rich, sweet fondues, such as caramel and butterscotch, are also scooped up avidly, but dessert fondues don't have to be calorie-laden to be enjoyable. Simple fruit purées, such as raspberry or plum, make excellent fondues.

The type of pot you will need depends on the type of fondue, but as a rule of thumb use the type of pot or substitute that you would for a cheese fondue, and keep the heat low. Chocolate scorches very easily so it is vital to use a special dessert fondue pot or a heavy enamelled cast-iron pot, the smaller the better, to minimise the surface area of chocolate that is exposed to the heat. Fruit purées could be made in a metal pot.

DIPPERS

As with savoury fondues, I aim to serve a variety of dippers – a few different fruits, two or three types of cake and perhaps a choice of two types of biscuit.

Fruits

Prepare fruits as near as possible to the time they will be needed. Arrange them attractively in groups on a dessert plate, or plates, depending on how many you are serving, and keep in a cool place, covered with cling film, until required. Fruits that discolour quickly, such as apples, pears and bananas, should be lightly brushed with lime, lemon or orange juice after they have been cut so that they keep their colour. Try to serve a selection of fruits; be creative and bear in mind how eye-catching they will look displayed on a plate for serving. Fruits to choose from include:

Apples
Choose tasty, juicy, eating apples. Peel and core them, cut into cubes and brush with lime, lemon or orange juice.

Cherries
Choose sweet, juicy cherries. Pit them using a cherry-stoner.

Figs
Choose ripe, but firm, green or black figs and cut them into quarters or sixths, depending on size.

Kiwi fruit
Peel, and cut the flesh into chunks.

Lychees
Peel and halve them and remove the stones.

Mango
Halve, then discard the stone. Peel the fruit and cut into chunks.

Mangosteens
Peel, remove the seeds and cut the flesh into largish pieces.

Oranges
Peel them, removing as much of the white pith as possible, then divide into segments.

Papaya
Halve, then scoop out and discard the seeds. Peel the fruit and cut into chunks.

Peaches and nectarines
Choose ripe but firm ones. Peel them or leave the skin on, as you prefer. Cut into cubes and brush with lime, lemon or orange juice.

Pears
Choose ripe but firm ones. Leave on the skin. Cut into cubes and brush with lime, lemon or orange juice.

Pineapple
Peel, slice, remove the core, then cut into chunks.

Plums
Halve them and remove the stones.

Rambutans
Peel, remove the stone and cut the flesh into largish pieces.

Seedless green or black grapes
Present them in small bunches.

Strawberries
Choose small ones and serve them with the hulls in.

Tangerines, satsumas, etc.
Peel and divide into segments.

Cake
You will need to choose cake that is not too delicate or crumbly, or it will disintegrate when swirled through the fondue. You must also be able to get a fork into it easily; meringues, for instance, are liable to shatter when you try to spear them.

The cake can be cut into bite-sized cubes, or baked in *petit four* cases (see page 94); not only do these look attractive, but they produce fewer crumbs.

Cut cake as near as possible to the time of serving it, then cover with cling film.

Biscuits
Finger-shaped biscuits are particularly appropriate. Bear in mind their fragility, and do not serve ones that are too big; it can be off-putting if someone dips a bitten-into biscuit into the fondue pot.

Arrange your choice of biscuits on plates as close as possible to the time of serving.

Marshmallows
Easy to spear on to a fork.

Chocolate Fondue

A simple chocolate fondue is probably the most commonly made dessert fondue, the richer the better. So, for the best results, use good-quality chocolate with 55–70 per cent cocoa solids.

―――――――― SERVES 6–8 ――――――――

350g (12oz) plain chocolate

25g (1oz) unsalted butter, chopped

300ml (½ pint) whipping cream

3 tablespoons brandy or rum

―――――――― TO SERVE ――――――――

fruit such as strawberries, chunks of pineapple and banana, wedges of plums, pears and peaches, orange segments, black cherries, lychees or mangosteens

marshmallows

Viennese Fingers (see page 142)

Mini Chocolate Cakes (see page 94)

Madeleines (see page 138)

1 Grate the chocolate into a fondue pot. Add the butter and heat very gently on the hob, stirring occasionally with a wooden spoon, until the chocolate has melted and the mixture is thick and smooth.

2 Add the cream and the brandy or rum. Transfer the pot to a burner. Serve the fondue with the fruit, marshmallows and other dippers.

VARIATIONS

Mint Chocolate Fondue
Use chocolates containing mint chips.

Orange Chocolate Fondue
Use orange-flavoured chocolate.

Fondue Fruit Fritters

FRUIT fritters are always popular, but they need to be eaten as soon as they are cooked, so the poor cook usually has a rough time, standing over a hot pot busily frying while everyone else sits around and eats the results of his or her labours. Fondue fruit fritters, where each person cooks their own helping, keep everyone happy. To make the fritters more special, sprinkle an appropriate liqueur on the fruit – Calvados on apples, kirsch on pineapple, orange liqueur or *eau-de-vie de fraises* on strawberries.

--- SERVES 6 ---

a selection of fresh fruit such as: 2 apples, cored and cut into chunks; 2 bananas, cut in 2.5cm (1 inch) pieces; 2 pineapples, peeled and cut into bite-sized pieces; quarters of fresh apricots, chunks of peaches, mangoes, papaya, nectarines, figs, kiwi fruit; small whole strawberries

olive oil for cooking

about 115g (4oz) caster sugar mixed with 1 teaspoon ground cinnamon

BATTER

115g (4oz) self-raising flour

a pinch of salt

15g (½oz) unsalted butter, melted

1 egg, separated

150ml (5fl oz) mixed milk and water

1 To make the batter, sift the flour and salt into a bowl and form a well in the centre. Add the butter, egg yolk and a little of the milk and water. Stir the ingredients together. When smooth, slowly pour in the remaining milk and water, stirring to keep the batter smooth. Leave for 30 minutes.

2 Prepare the fruit as necessary.

3 Whisk the egg white until it stands in soft peaks, then gently fold into the batter.

4 Pour enough olive oil to half-fill a fondue pot into a saucepan on the hob and heat to 190°C/375°F. Carefully pour the oil into a warmed fondue pot, put over a burner and reheat.

5 Spear the fruit on to long-handled forks and swirl in the batter, allowing the excess to flow off, then cook the fruit until crisp and golden. Drain briefly on paper towels, then dip the cooked fruit in the cinnamon sugar and eat.

Mars Bar Fondue

COMMERCIAL Mars Bar ice cream became very popular in the mid-1990s, but 30 years earlier we had discovered that simple frozen Mars Bars were delicious. We also discovered Mars Bars could be melted to make an excellent fondue.

―――――――――――― SERVES 4 ――――――――――――

2 Mars Bars

115g (4oz) plain chocolate

150ml (5fl oz) double cream

―――――――――――― TO SERVE ――――――――――――

strawberries

tangerine segments

dark cherries

chunks of kiwi fruit

Sponge Fingers (see page 139)

1 Coarsely chop the Mars Bars and chocolate and put into a fondue pot placed over a saucepan of simmering water.

2 Add the cream and heat gently, stirring from time to time, until the mixture is smooth.

3 Transfer the pot to a burner. Serve the fondue with the fruit and sponge fingers.

Mocha Fondue

THE flavours of chocolate and coffee enhance each other and make a delicious, rich-tasting fondue.

SERVES 4

225g (½lb) good-quality plain chocolate
150ml (5fl oz) double cream

about 4 tablespoons Tia Maria or other
coffee liqueur, to taste

TO SERVE
---

stoned black cherries

chunks of banana and pear (dipped in lemon juice)

peach or nectarine slices

strawberries

mangosteens, lychees, or rambutans

marshmallows

Sponge Fingers (see page 139)

Langues de Chat (see page 140)

Madeleines (see page 138)

---

1 Grate the chocolate into a fondue pot. Add the cream and put over a burner. Heat gently, stirring, until the chocolate has melted.

2 Stir in the Tia Maria or other liqueur to taste. Serve with the fruit, marshmallows and other dippers.

Apricot Fondue

*T*HIS fruity fondue is cooked partly on top of the stove and partly over a fondue burner. The basic apricot purée can be made well in advance.

SERVES 4–6

450g (1lb) dried apricots

about 50g (2oz) caster sugar, to taste

150ml (5fl oz) double cream

3 tablespoons apricot brandy

lemon juice, to taste

1 tablespoon chopped almonds

1 tablespoon chopped walnuts

TO SERVE

chunks of mango and papaya

orange segments

cubes of Sponge Cake (see page 141)

sliced bananas (dipped in lemon juice)

strawberries

Sponge Fingers (see page 139)

Madeleines (see page 138)

1 Soak the apricots overnight in enough water to cover. Transfer the apricots and liquid to a heavy-based saucepan, stir in the sugar and cook gently for about 25 minutes or until tender.

2 Pour the contents of the saucepan into a blender and mix to a purée. Pour into a fondue pot. Stir in the cream and apricot brandy, and add lemon juice to taste to lift the flavour. Add the nuts.

3 Put the fondue pot over a burner and gently heat the apricot mixture, stirring frequently with a wooden spoon, for about 3 minutes. Serve the fondue with the fruit and other dippers.

Zabaglione Fondue

I*T* is better to make zabaglione on the hob than over a fondue burner; once the zabaglione is ready, it can be transferred to the burner. Traditional zabaglione is very sweet and rich. It is made with Marsala, a very sweet, fortified wine, but I've used dry sherry and dry white wine for a lighter result. For an even lighter result, use 3 whole eggs instead of egg yolks. Zabaglione does take a little time to prepare, so your guests will have a short intermission in their meal.

SERVES 4

---

4 egg yolks

2 tablespoons caster sugar, preferably vanilla-flavoured

2 tablespoons dry sherry

2 tablespoons dry white wine

TO SERVE

---

whole small strawberries

chunks of peach and fig

Sponge Fingers (see page 139)

---

1 Whisk the egg yolks with the sugar in a glass or stainless-steel bowl.

2 Put the bowl over a saucepan of very hot, but not boiling, water and whisk, preferably with an electric whisk, adding the sherry and wine as you go, until the mixture is very light and will hold its shape.

3 Pour the zabaglione into a fondue pot, put over a burner and start dipping.

Cointreau Fondue

*T*HE fondue can be made in advance, either in a fondue pot or in a saucepan, and kept warm in a bowl or larger saucepan of hot water, with a disc of greaseproof paper closely covering its surface.

SERVES 4

2 large egg yolks

50g (2oz) caster sugar, preferably vanilla-flavoured

225ml (8fl oz) milk

finely grated rind of 1 orange

2 tablespoons Cointreau or other orange-flavoured liqueur

TO SERVE

whole small strawberries

chunks of pear (brushed with lemon juice), figs and mango

seedless green grapes

Sponge Fingers (see page 139)

Langues de Chat (see page 140)

1 Whisk the egg yolks and sugar together until thick.

2 Heat the milk to simmering point in a fondue pot. Pour on to the egg yolk mixture, whisking at the same time. Pour the mixture back into the fondue pot and cook over a low heat, stirring with a wooden spoon, until the sauce is thick enough to coat the back of the spoon.

3 Stir in the orange rind and Cointreau and start dipping.

Marshmallow Fondue

I had a packet of marshmallows in the cupboard for a long time because I did not know what to do with them. Then a friend suggested this recipe. It was a great success.

SERVES 6

450ml (16fl oz) single cream
2 tablespoons cornflour

175g (6oz) marshmallows

TO SERVE

chunks of pineapple
whole small strawberries

Chocolate Viennese Fingers
(see page 142)
Mini Chocolate Cakes (see page 94)

1 Pour most of the cream into a saucepan, preferably non-stick, and bring to the boil.

2 In a bowl, blend the remaining cream with the cornflour. Pour the boiling cream on to the cream and cornflour mixture, stirring. Pour back into the saucepan and heat, stirring, until thickened.

3 Stir in the marshmallows until melted.

4 Pour into a fondue pot, put over a burner, and serve with the fruit and other dippers.

Maple Fudge Fondue

MAPLE syrup adds its characteristic rich flavour to this fondue, which is a delight to those with a sweet tooth.

SERVES 4

75g (3oz) unsalted butter

150g (5oz) light brown sugar

2 tablespoons maple syrup

75ml (3fl oz) crème fraîche

TO SERVE
---

chunks of pear (brushed with lemon juice)

whole small strawberries

chunks of plum

chunks of apricot

cubes of Sponge Cake (see page 141)

1 Melt the butter in a fondue pot, then add the sugar and maple syrup. Heat gently, stirring occasionally, until the sugar has dissolved completely.

2 Stir in the crème fraîche and bring to the boil. Serve with the fruit and cubes of sponge cake.

Peppermint Fondue with Mini Chocolate Cakes

THE chocolate cakes are baked in *petit four* cases to make bite-sized mouthfuls. I usually remove the paper cases before serving them, but you can leave your guests to do it.

SERVES 6

570ml (1 pint) single cream

2 tablespoons cornflour

115g (4oz) icing sugar

crème de menthe or a few drops of peppermint essence, to taste

MINI CHOCOLATE CAKES (makes 32)

2 tablespoons cocoa powder

40g (1½oz) butter or margarine

40g (1½oz) caster sugar

1 egg, beaten

40g (1½oz) self-raising flour

a pinch of baking powder

---

1 To make the chocolate cakes, preheat the oven to 180°C/350°F/ Gas Mark 4. Blend the cocoa powder with 2 teaspoons of hot water. Beat the butter or margarine with the sugar until soft and light. Gradually beat in the egg, beating well after each addition. Sift the flour and baking powder over the egg mixture, then gently fold in using a metal spoon until just evenly mixed. Add the cocoa powder mixture towards the end.

2 Put teaspoons of the cake mixture into 32 *petit four* cases on a baking sheet and bake for 10–15 minutes until the cakes have risen and a skewer inserted in the centre of one of them comes out clean.

3 Transfer the cases to a wire rack and leave to cool.

4 Pour most of the cream into a saucepan, preferably non-stick, and bring to the boil.

5 Meanwhile, in a bowl, blend the remaining cream into the cornflour. Pour the boiling cream on to the cream and cornflour mixture, stirring. Pour back into the saucepan, add the sugar and cook, stirring, until the sauce thickens. Add crème de menthe or peppermint essence to taste.

6 Pour into a fondue pot and reheat over a burner. Serve with the Mini Chocolate Cakes.

Caramel Fondue

*T*HIS rich, sweet fondue takes about 10 minutes to make, but it keeps warm beautifully so you can make it before the meal begins. I make it on the hob, then transfer it to a fondue pot to serve.

SERVES 4

150g (5oz) unsalted butter
150g (5oz) sugar
1½ tablespoons golden syrup

6 tablespoons milk
a few drops of vanilla essence

TO SERVE

chunks of apricot
chunks of peach
pineapple cubes
whole small strawberries

cubes of Sponge Cake (see page 141)
Madeleines (see page 138)
Viennese Fingers (see page 142)

1 Put all the ingredients in a saucepan, preferably non-stick, and stir over a low heat until the butter has melted and the sugar dissolved.

2 Bring to the boil and boil, stirring, for 5 minutes.

3 Pour into a warmed fondue pot, scraping out as much of the mixture as possible. Put over a burner and reheat. Serve with the fruit and other dippers.

Mixed Fruit Platter with Ginger and Lime Dip

*T*HIS is not a true fondue, but a cold dip served with fresh fruit. It satisfies both those who like to end a meal with something creamy and those who prefer something refreshing. You can use low-, medium- or full-fat soft cheese. Provide cocktail sticks and/ or forks for the fruits.

SERVES 6

2 large oranges, peeled
225g (½lb) seedless white grapes
1 ogen melon, cut into bite-sized chunks

½ cantaloup melon, cut into bite-sized chunks
½ watermelon, scooped into balls
1 peach, cut into wedges

GINGER AND LIME DIP

115g (4oz) soft cheese
300ml (½ pint) Greek yogurt
2 tablespoons lime marmalade

1 teaspoon finely grated lime rind
2 teaspoons chopped cystallised ginger
finely grated lemon rind, for decoration

1 To make the dip, put the soft cheese into a bowl and beat until smooth, very soft and fluffy.

2 Beat in the yogurt, marmalade and lime rind. Stir in the ginger.

3 Spoon into a suitable serving bowl, cover and chill for 1 hour.

4 Divide the oranges into segments. Arrange on a large serving plate with the remaining fruit. Cover with cling film and chill until required.

5 Sprinkle the lemon rind over the surface of the dip. Serve with the fruit.

Butterscotch Fondue

*T*HE rum is a must for this fondue because it gives a properly balanced flavour. It is a good idea to cover your hand when adding the golden syrup and cream to the caramel, in case of spitting.

SERVES 4–6

50g (2oz) unsalted butter, chopped

115g (4oz) demerara sugar

2 tablespoons golden syrup

300ml (½ pint) double cream

3 tablespoons rum

TO SERVE

chunks of apple (brushed with lemon juice)

pineapple cubes

orange or mandarin segments

seedless green grapes

cubes of Sponge Cake (see page 141)

Sponge Fingers (see page 139)

Viennese Fingers (see page 142)

1 Put the butter and sugar in a heavy-based saucepan, preferably non-stick, and heat gently, stirring occasionally, until the sugar has dissolved. Continue to cook without stirring until it is a rich caramel.

2 Immediately remove the pan from the heat and add the golden syrup and cream. Return to the heat, stir to dissolve the caramel, and bring to the boil.

3 Pour into a warmed fondue pot, taking care to scrape as much of the mixture as possible from the saucepan. Put over a fondue burner, add the rum and reheat. Serve with the fruit and other dippers.

Chocolate, Honey and Hazelnut Fondue

*T*HIS fondue is lightly sweetened with honey, which adds its own flavour. Just how much honey you use depends on how sweet you want the fondue to be, and how dominant the taste of honey.

SERVES 4

50g (2oz) hazelnuts

300g (10oz) plain chocolate

2–3 tablespoons clear honey, to taste

300ml (½ pint) whipping cream

TO SERVE

apple wedges (brushed with lemon juice)

slices of pear (brushed with lemon juice)

orange segments

quarters of fresh apricot

seedless grapes

cubes of Sponge Cake (see page 141)

Viennese Fingers (see page 142)

1 Preheat the grill. Toast the hazelnuts until the skins dry and split and the nuts are lightly browned. Leave the nuts to cool slightly, then rub off the skins. Put the nuts into a grinder, small blender or food processor and grind them.

2 Grate the chocolate into a fondue pot. Add the honey and cream. Heat very gently, stirring frequently with a wooden spoon, until the mixture is smooth. Stir in the hazelnuts. Serve with the fruit and other dippers.

Cinnamon and Lemon Fondue Fritters

*T*HESE fritters are made with choux pastry, so have the flour by the side of the hob ready to be shot into the pan in one go. You can make the pastry in advance – drop teaspoons of the choux mixture on to a baking sheet and freeze them. Allow them to thaw in the refrigerator, then transfer to room temperature 20 minutes before they will be cooked.

SERVES 4

6 tablespoons milk	90g (3½oz) plain flour
grated rind and juice of 1 lemon	2 eggs
40g (1½oz) butter	1 teaspoon ground cinnamon
150g (5oz) caster sugar	oil for deep frying

1 Put the milk, lemon rind, butter and 25g (1oz) of the sugar in a small non-stick saucepan. Heat gently, stirring, until the sugar has dissolved. Increase the heat and quickly bring to the boil.

2 Quickly remove the pan from the heat and add all the flour in one go and the lemon juice, stirring constantly with a wooden spoon until the mixture is smooth. Return the pan to a low heat and cook, stirring, until the mixture leaves the sides of the pan clean.

3 Leave the mixture to cool slightly then gradually beat in the eggs, beating well after each addition so that the mixture is stiff.

4 Mix the remaining sugar with the cinnamon.

5 Pour enough oil to half-fill a fondue pot into a saucepan on the hob and heat to 190°C/375°F. Carefully pour the oil into a warmed fondue pot, put over a burner and reheat the oil to 180°C/350°F.

6 Drop teaspoons of the choux mixture into the hot oil and cook until golden. Scoop out with a slotted spoon or Chinese wire strainer and touch on to paper towels to drain. Roll the hot fritters in the cinnamon sugar.

Accompaniments

It is well worth spending time choosing an interesting and varied selection of dips, sauces, relishes, breads, salads, etc. to accompany a fondue; they can turn an ordinary fondue party into a truly memorable occasion. Consider the overall appearance of the spread, as well as the compatibility of the accompaniments with each other and the fondue.

I have provided a variety of bread recipes that are very easy to make (forget what you might have heard about bread needing to have just the right temperature or it will not rise). Keep a couple of loaves in the freezer so that you have some to hand should you decide to have an impromptu party. If you buy loaves for a cheese fondue you will need to exercise some caution; much commercially produced bread contains a lot of water, which makes it very light and soft-textured. Firmer, drier bread is preferable – unless you want much forfeit-paying.

DIPS AND SAUCES

Thai-Style Ginger Dip

YOU can adjust the levels of the ingredients to suit your taste, and try adding other flavourings, such as sesame oil and chopped coriander.

SERVES 6

2.5cm (1 inch) piece of ginger, grated

1 small clove garlic, finely crushed

2 spring onions, finely chopped

2 tablespoons soy sauce

6 tablespoons rice vinegar

2 teaspoons sugar

finely chopped, seeded red chilli, to garnish

1 Put the ginger, garlic, spring onions, soy sauce, rice vinegar and sugar in a bowl and whisk together.

2 Leave to stand, stirring occasionally, until the sugar has dissolved.

3 Sprinkle the red chilli over the dip to serve.

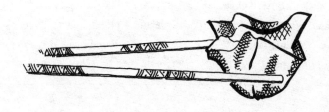

Szechuan Dipping Sauce

I usually serve each bowl of this dip with a coriander leaf floating on the top.

___
SERVES 4–6
___

115ml (4fl oz) soy sauce

2 tablespoons finely chopped spring onions

1 clove garlic, crushed and finely chopped

½ teaspoon grated fresh ginger

1½ teaspoons white wine vinegar

2 teaspoons sesame oil

a few drops of Tabasco sauce, to taste

Stir all the ingredients together.

Sesame-Ginger Dipping Sauce

*T*HIS convergence of Eastern and Western ingredients works extremely well.

___
SERVES 4–6
___

1 clove garlic, finely crushed

2–3 teaspoons grated fresh ginger

4 tablespoons sesame oil

1 tablespoon balsamic vinegar

1 tablespoon lime juice

1 tablespoon rice wine

175ml (6fl oz) Greek yogurt

about 1 tablespoon soy sauce

freshly ground black pepper

1 Stir the garlic, ginger, sesame oil, balsamic vinegar, lime juice and rice wine into the yogurt.

2 Add soy sauce and pepper to taste.

Curry Dipping Sauce

*U*SE your favourite curry powder or paste, whether it is hot, or mild Indian curry powder or a green or red Thai curry paste.

SERVES ABOUT 6

about 1½–2½ teaspoons curry powder or paste, to taste

1¼ teaspoons ground ginger

¼ teaspoon paprika

½ teaspoon turmeric

175ml (6fl oz) mayonnaise

175ml (6fl oz) Greek yogurt

about ½ teaspoon chilli powder

salt and freshly ground black pepper

1 Stir the curry powder or paste, ginger, paprika, turmeric and mayonnaise into the yogurt.

2 Add chilli powder, salt and pepper to taste. Adjust the level of curry powder or paste, if necessary.

Horseradish Dipping Sauce

*T*AKE care when peeling and grating horseradish as it can sting the eyes. If you do not have any freshly grated horseradish, use 1½–2 tablespoons prepared horseradish.

SERVES 4–6

3 tablespoons grated fresh horseradish

2 tablespoons olive oil

2 tablespoons sherry vinegar

1 teaspoon soy sauce

4 tablespoons soured cream

salt and freshly ground black pepper

Whisk the horseradish, oil, vinegar, soy sauce and 2 tablespoons water into the soured cream until smooth. Season to taste.

Hot Sweet and Sour Dipping Sauce

*T*HE dressing can be made in advance up to the end of step 2, and kept covered in the refrigerator, but it is best not to add the coriander leaves and cucumber until just before serving.

SERVES 4–6

a pinch of dried chilli flakes

1 teaspoon finely crushed garlic

1 teaspoon finely chopped coriander stem

150ml (5fl oz) rice vinegar

25g (1oz) soft brown sugar

25g (1oz) caster sugar

1 tablespoon chopped coriander leaves

¼ cucumber, seeded and finely chopped

salt

1 Put the first six ingredients into a saucepan with 4 tablespoons water and heat, stirring, until the sugars have dissolved.

2 Bring to the boil, then leave to cool.

3 Add the coriander leaves and cucumber, and salt to taste.

Mayonnaise

BLENDERS and food processors have revolutionised mayonnaise-making. Now it is child's play to whip up a batch of home-made mayo in a matter of a few minutes. It lends itself to innumerable different flavouring possibilities: all will improve if left to stand for at least 30 minutes before serving.

SERVES 4–6; MAKES 350ML (12FL OZ)

2 egg yolks (medium)

1 teaspoon Dijon mustard

2 tablespoons white wine vinegar or 1 tablespoon lemon juice

300ml (½ pint) olive oil

salt and freshly ground white pepper

1 Put the egg yolks, mustard and half the vinegar or lemon juice into a blender or food processor. Mix briefly.

2 With the motor running, very slowly pour in the oil in a thin steady stream until about half the oil has been added, then increase the speed slightly and slowly pour in the remaining oil.

3 Add the rest of the vinegar or lemon juice and seasoning to taste.

VARIATIONS

Tartare Sauce
Add 2 tablespoons small capers, 1½ tablespoons each chopped gherkins and parsley, 2 teaspoons chopped chives and 2 table-spoons lemon juice to 350ml (12fl oz) homemade or bottled mayonnaise.

Extra Light Mayonnaise
Whisk 1–2 egg whites until they form stiff peaks, then fold into 350ml (12fl oz) home-made Mayonnaise or bottled mayonnaise.

Light Mayonnaise
Stir together natural Greek yogurt or plain yogurt and home-made or bottled mayonnaise; the proportions will depend on how light you want the dressing to be.

Chantilly Mayonnaise
Whip 75ml (3fl oz) whipping or double cream until it stands in soft peaks, then gently fold it into 350ml (12fl oz) home-made Mayonnaise or bottled mayonnaise.

Watercress Mayonnaise
Remove the tough stalks from a bunch of watercress. Chop the leaves and fine stems and add to 350ml (12fl oz) home-made Mayonnaise or bottled mayonnaise.

Lemon Mayonnaise
If making home-made Mayonnaise, use lemon juice rather than vinegar, and add 2 tablespoons finely grated lemon rind to the egg yolks. If using bottled mayonnaise, add the grated lemon rind to the mayonnaise.

Horseradish Mayonnaise
Add 1–2 tablespoons lemon juice and 2 tablespoons freshly grated horseradish to 350ml (12fl oz) home-made Mayonnaise or bottled mayonnaise.

Herb Mayonnaise
Add about 6 tablespoons chopped herbs to 350ml (12fl oz) home-made Mayonnaise or bottled mayonnaise.

Caper Mayonnaise
Add 4 teaspoons chopped capers and 1 teaspoon tarragon vinegar to 350ml (12fl oz) home-made Mayonnaise or bottled mayonnaise.

Roast Garlic Mayonnaise
Roasting garlic softens its flavour and gives it a delicious smoky taste, which, in turn, adds an enticing flavour to the mayonnaise. If liked, 2 mashed anchovy fillets can be added with the egg yolks.

Put 2 unpeeled garlic bulbs on individual pieces of greaseproof paper, lay a sprig of thyme or rosemary on each and trickle over 1 tablespoon of olive oil. Fold over the paper and seal the edges tightly to make neat parcels, then put them on a baking sheet and bake at 180°C/350°F/Gas Mark 4 for 35–40 minutes, until the garlic is soft. Allow the garlic to cool slightly, then squeeze the cloves from their skins into a blender. Make the mayonnaise, following the method in the main recipe, with 2 egg yolks, 2–3 teaspoons lemon juice, 300ml (½ pint) virgin olive oil and salt and freshly ground black pepper.

Saffron Mayonnaise
Infuse a pinch of crushed saffron strands in 1½ tablespoons lemon juice for about 5 minutes. Make the mayonnaise as in the main recipe.

Ginger and Spring Onion Mayonnaise
Add ½ teaspoon ginger juice (made by squeezing a piece of fresh ginger in a garlic press) and 3–4 tablespoons very finely chopped spring onions to 350ml (12fl oz) home-made Mayonnaise made with 150ml (5fl oz) olive oil and 150ml (5fl oz) peanut (groundnut) oil.

Sesame and Garlic Mayonnaise
Add 2 crushed garlic cloves, 2 tablespoons very finely chopped spring onions and 1 tablespoon toasted sesame seeds to 350ml (12fl oz) home-made Mayonnaise made with 150ml (5fl oz) olive oil and 150ml (5fl oz) peanut (groundnut) oil.

Curry Mayonnaise
Mix together 6 tablespoons home-made Mayonnaise or bottled mayonnaise, 6 tablespoons double cream, 1 tablespoon curry paste, 1 tablespoon finely chopped shallot or red onion, the juice of ½ lemon and 1 tablespoon mango chutney.

Sun-Dried Tomato Aïoli

*T*HIS is a type of mayonnaise that is flavoured with garlic and sun-dried tomatoes. Any that is not eaten can be stored in a covered container in the refrigerator for 3–4 days.

———————————————— SERVES 6 ————————————————

3 plump cloves garlic, halved lengthways

salt and freshly ground black pepper

2 large egg yolks

350ml (12fl oz) olive oil

4–5 sun-dried tomatoes packed in oil, drained and chopped

about 1 tablespoon lime or lemon juice

1 Put the garlic, a pinch of salt and the egg yolks in a blender or food processor. Mix together.

2 With the motor running, very slowly pour in the oil until it has all been added and the dip is very thick.

3 Transfer the dip to a bowl and add the sun-dried tomatoes, and lime or lemon juice and seasoning to taste.

Oriental Tartare Sauce

*T*HE sauce can be stored, covered, in the refrigerator for up to one week.

———————————————— SERVES 4 ————————————————

1 egg

1 small clove garlic

½ teaspoon mustard powder

175ml (6fl oz) mild olive oil

4 small gherkins, finely chopped

1½ tablespoons chopped coriander

1½ tablespoons small capers

2 teaspoons lime juice, or to taste

salt and freshly ground black pepper

1 Put the egg, garlic and mustard into a blender or food processor. With the motor running, slowly pour in the oil in a steady trickle to produce a thick sauce.

2 Transfer the sauce to a bowl and stir in the gherkins, coriander and capers. Add lime juice and seasoning to taste.

Rémoulade Sauce

RÉMOULADE sauce is a piquant mayonnaise-like mixture flavoured with mustard, capers, gherkins, anchovies and herbs.

SERVES 6

2 egg yolks	425ml (15fl oz) virgin olive oil
1½ teaspoons Dijon mustard	3 tablespoons lemon juice
8 anchovy fillets, rinsed	1 tablespoon chopped gherkins
2½ tablespoons chopped basil leaves	2 teaspoons torn basil leaves
25g (1oz) plus 1 tablespoon capers	freshly ground black pepper

1 Put the egg yolks, mustard, anchovy fillets, chopped basil and 25g (1oz) capers into a blender or food processor and mix briefly. With the motor running, very slowly pour in the oil until all the oil has been added and the sauce is thick.

2 Briefly mix in the lemon juice and plenty of black pepper.

3 Turn the sauce into a bowl and stir in the 1 tablespoon capers, the gherkins and the torn basil leaves.

Oriental Mustard Sauce

SOME sesame oils are made from toasted sesame seeds, so are dark in colour and very richly flavoured; they are not the type for this sauce.

SERVES 4

150ml (5fl oz) sesame oil

2 tablespoons rice vinegar

1 tablespoon mirin or dry sherry

150ml (5fl oz) Dijon mustard

2 tablespoons chopped spring onions

3 tablespoons coriander leaves, chopped

salt and freshly ground black pepper

1 Stir the sesame oil, rice vinegar and mirin or dry sherry into the mustard until thoroughly combined.

2 Stir in the spring onions and coriander leaves and season to taste.

3 Keep covered in the refrigerator until required

Mediterranean Dip

*I*F you are unable to find black olives packed in oil, or have not packed any in oil yourself, leave the olives to macerate in the 115ml (4fl oz) olive oil for at least several hours; drain the oil from the olives, then use the olives and oil according to the recipe. Any leftover dip can be kept, covered, in the refrigerator for up to a week. As well as being used as a dip, it can be spread sparingly on bread or pizza bases, or tossed with pasta or rice, with plenty of freshly grated Parmesan cheese.

SERVES 4–6

50g (2oz) can of anchovy fillets, drained

2 cloves garlic, chopped

20g (2oz) sun-dried tomatoes in olive oil, drained

115g (4oz) pitted black olives packed in oil, drained

2 teaspoons Dijon mustard

2 egg yolks

115ml (4fl oz) olive oil

2 teaspoons lemon juice

salt and freshly ground black pepper

1 Soak the anchovy fillets in water for about 20 minutes. Drain off and discard the water. Chop the fillets and put into a blender or food processor.

2 Add the garlic, sun-dried tomatoes, olives and mustard and process until just coarsely chopped.

3 Add the egg yolks, process briefly, then, with the motor running, pour in the oil in a slow steady stream. The finished dip should be nubbly rather than smooth. Add the lemon juice and seasoning to taste.

4 Transfer to a bowl, cover and leave in a cool place for several hours, preferably overnight.

Piquant Dip

*I*NSTEAD of using oil, you could use 150ml (5fl oz) double cream.

SERVES 4–6

1 hardboiled egg yolk

1-2 teaspoons Dijon mustard

150ml (5fl oz) mild olive oil or mixed olive and vegetable oil

1 gherkin, finely chopped

1 tablespoon capers

about 1 teaspoon *fines herbes*

salt and freshly ground black pepper

1 Mash the egg yolk with the mustard. Slowly pour in the oil, beating constantly.

2 Add the gherkin, capers and *fines herbes*. Season to taste.

Coriander and Ginger Pesto

*T*O keep the pesto for a few days, pour a thin layer of oil over the surface and store in the refrigerator; stir before serving.

SERVES 4–6

50g (2oz) coriander leaves

50g (2oz) cashew nuts

2 cloves garlic, chopped

2 tablespoons grated fresh ginger

175-225ml (6-8fl oz) olive oil

juice of ½ lime, to taste

salt and freshly ground black pepper

1 Put the coriander, cashew nuts, garlic and ginger in a blender or food processor.

2 With the motor running, slowly pour in enough of the oil in a thin steady stream to make a loose, smooth cream. Add lime juice and seasoning to taste.

Grilled Red Pepper Sauce

*T*HE sauce can be made a day or so in advance and stored, covered, in the refrigerator.

SERVES 4–6

4 red peppers	1 red chilli, seeded and chopped
4 cloves garlic, unpeeled	1 tablespoon paprika
about 4 tablespoons extra virgin olive oil	2 teaspoons balsamic vinegar
4 shallots	salt and freshly ground black pepper

1 Preheat the grill. Brush the peppers and garlic with some of the oil. Grill, turning the peppers frequently so that they cook evenly, until their skin is charred and blistered and they have collapsed. Remove the garlic cloves when they have softened, and peel them.

2 Leave the peppers until they are cool enough to handle, then, working over a bowl to catch any juices, peel away the skins and remove and discard the seeds and cores.

3 Put the peppers, garlic and juices in a blender or food processor.

4 Meanwhile, heat 1 tablespoon of the remaining oil in a frying pan and fry the shallots and chilli until softened. Stir in the paprika for 1 minute. Add to the blender or food processor with the vinegar and 2 tablespoons of the oil. Process to a purée. Season to taste, and pass through a sieve, if liked.

SALSAS AND RELISHES

Red and Yellow Pepper Relish

*T*HE combination of red and yellow pepper strips looks attractive, but if you cannot get yellow peppers, don't worry – simply use four red peppers. Don't on any account substitute green peppers for the yellow ones.

SERVES 4–6

2 large red peppers, sliced lengthways into thin strips

2 large yellow peppers, sliced lengthways into thin strips

1 small onion, finely chopped

50ml (2fl oz) white wine vinegar

1½ teaspoons sugar

1 teaspoon mustard powder, to taste

salt and freshly ground black pepper

1 Put the pepper strips, onion, vinegar and sugar in a saucepan with 75ml (3fl oz) water. Stir over a low heat until the sugar has dissolved, then simmer until the mixture is reduced by a half and has a dryish consistency.

2 Add mustard and seasoning to taste, then transfer to a bowl. Leave to cool, then cover and place in the refrigerator until 30 minutes before required.

Oriental-Style Aubergine Relish

THE relish can be made two or three days in advance. After it has cooled for 1 hour, cover it and keep it in the refrigerator; return to cool room temperature 30 minutes before serving.

SERVES 6

3 large aubergines

2 tablespoons sesame oil

1 red pepper, halved lengthways

3 tablespoons olive oil

½ red onion, finely diced

2 cloves garlic, finely diced

1 small red chilli, seeded and finely chopped

1 teaspoon grated fresh ginger

4 spring onions, thinly sliced

2 tablespoons finely chopped coriander

salt and freshly ground black pepper

1 Preheat the grill. Preheat the oven to 190°C/375°F/Gas Mark 5. Prick the aubergines with a fork and brush with the sesame oil. Bake for about 30 minutes until soft.

2 Meanwhile, grill the pepper until charred and blistered all over. Leave until cool enough to handle, then remove the skin. Cut the pepper into dice.

3 Heat the olive oil and fry the red onion, garlic, chilli and ginger until soft but not brown.

4 Cut the aubergines in half lengthways and scoop the flesh into a food processor. Add the red onion mixture and mix together. Turn into a bowl.

5 Mix the red pepper, spring onions and coriander into the aubergine mixture and season to taste. Cover and leave in a cool place for at least 2 hours. Serve at room temperature.

Avocado Salsa

YOU need firm tomatoes for this recipe. If you leave them in the water for too long when peeling them, the flesh will begin to soften. Keep their juice and seeds for casseroles, soups, sauces and salad dressings – they are full of flavour. The salsa can be made up to the end of Step 3 several hours in advance and kept in a cool place – the flavour will be all the better for it. I advise making the salsa, up to the end of stage 2, ahead of time if possible, because it does taste better. But the avocado should not be added until about 1 hour before the meal is to be eaten.

SERVES 4

2 large, well-flavoured firm tomatoes	1½ tablespoons chopped coriander
½ clove garlic, crushed and very finely chopped	a few drops of chilli sauce or a pinch of dried chilli flakes
2 tablespoons lime juice	salt and freshly ground black pepper
½ red onion, very finely chopped	1 avocado

1 Lightly mark a cross with the point of a sharp knife in the rounded end of each tomato, put in a heatproof bowl and pour over boiling water. Leave for 8–15 seconds then remove with a slotted spoon. When cool enough to handle, peel off the skins. Cut the tomatoes in half and, using a teaspoon, scoop out the seeds. Finely chop the flesh and put it in a bowl.

2 Add the garlic, lime juice, red onion, coriander, chilli sauce or chilli flakes and seasoning.

3 Halve the avocado lengthways, discard the stone, then cut each half in half. Peel off the skin and dice the flesh. Stir into the tomato mixture.

4 Cover and leave for an hour.

Grilled Sweetcorn Salsa

GRILLING brings out the sweetness of the sweetcorn and adds a new dimension to it.

SERVES 4

2 sweetcorn cobs

olive oil, for brushing

2 large, well-flavoured tomatoes, skinned, seeded and finely chopped (see page 116)

½ red onion, very finely chopped

½ red pepper, finely chopped

a pinch of dried chilli flakes

1½–2 tablespoons lime juice

2 tablespoons chopped coriander

salt and freshly ground black pepper

1 Preheat the grill. Lightly brush the sweetcorn with olive oil and grill for about 8 minutes, turning frequently so that the cobs cook evenly.

2 Leave until cool enough to handle, then, using a large sharp knife, scrape the kernels into a bowl.

3 Mix the remaining ingredients with the kernels, cover and leave for 2–3 hours, if possible.

SALADS AND VEGETABLES

Potato, Peanut and Coriander Salad

SOME people suffer very severe allergic reactions to peanuts so, unless you are sure none of your guests are affected, it is worth mentioning that this salad contains them. Any leftover salad can be kept covered in the refrigerator for a day or so.

SERVES 6

700g (1½lb) new potatoes or salad potatoes

2 sprigs of coriander

6 spring onions, finely chopped

DRESSING

5 tablespoons groundnut (peanut) oil
finely grated rind and juice of 1 lime

2½ tablespoons coarsely chopped coriander

about 50g (2oz) unsalted peanuts, chopped

salt and freshly ground black pepper

1 Cook the potatoes with the coriander sprigs in boiling salted water until tender. Drain well and discard the coriander. Cut the potatoes into small chunks.

2 Meanwhile, shake the dressing ingredients together in a screw-top jar.

3 Toss the warm potatoes with the dressing and the spring onions. Leave to cool.

4 Just before serving, toss the chopped coriander and peanuts with the potatoes.

Green, Red and White Salad

*T*HIS salad looks very effective when presented in a bowl on the table.

───────────────── SERVES 6 ─────────────────

2 red peppers, halved lengthways

1 large cauliflower, separated into florets

450g (1lb) broccoli, separated into florets

DRESSING

115ml (4fl oz) extra virgin olive oil

1 heaped tablespoon wholegrain mustard

leaves from 15g (½oz) bunch of tarragon

2 cloves garlic, finely crushed

a dash of balsamic vinegar

a dash of Tabasco (optional)

salt and freshly ground black pepper

1 Preheat the grill. Grill the red peppers until evenly charred and blistered. When cool enough to handle, remove the charred skin and slice the peppers into thin strips.

2 Blanch the cauliflower and broccoli in a large saucepan of boiling water for about 1 minute until tender but still firm. Drain and rinse under running cold water. Drain well.

3 Whisk all the dressing ingredients together.

4 Toss together the cauliflower, broccoli and red pepper strips.

5 Pour the dressing over the salad and toss to coat.

Crisp Green Salad

*T*HIS is an all-purpose green salad that will accompany many different fondue recipes. It is important to choose a small selection of different leaves to give a variety of tastes, colours and textures, tossed with a dressing of flavourful oil, a few fresh herbs and a little good vinegar. (A little mustard in the dressing will help to keep it emulsified if you make it in advance.) If your salad leaves aren't crisp, rinse them in cold water and shake or pat them dry, then put them in a polythene bag and refrigerate for 1 hour.

SERVES 4

1 shallot, finely chopped	6 handfuls of mixed salad leaves
1½ tablespoons sherry vinegar or white wine vinegar	a small handful of fresh herbs such as parsley, thyme, basil, lovage, chervil and/or marjoram, chopped
5-6 tablespoons virgin or extra virgin olive oil	salt and freshly ground black pepper

1 Combine the shallot, vinegar and seasoning then whisk in the olive oil. Taste and adjust the levels of vinegar and olive oil, if necessary.

2 Put the salad leaves in a bowl, scatter over the herbs and toss.

3 Immediately before serving, pour over the dressing and toss gently but thoroughly.

Tomato Salad

*T*HIS salad calls for finely chopped tomatoes so it can be easily eaten with just a fork.

10 well-flavoured plum tomatoes, peeled, seeded and finely chopped

1 tablespoon finely diced red onion

8 basil leaves, torn into shreds

2 tablespoons extra virgin olive oil

1 teaspoon sherry vinegar

coarse sea salt and freshly ground black pepper

1 Put the tomatoes in a serving dish. Scatter over the red onion and basil leaves.

2 Whisk together the olive oil and vinegar. Pour over the tomatoes. Season with coarse sea salt and plenty of pepper. Cover and leave for 1–2 hours.

Spinach and Chicory Salad

*I*T is important to use small spinach leaves because the flavour of large ones is too strong and coarse.

SERVES 4–6

3 heads of chicory

DRESSING

115ml (4fl oz) extra virgin olive oil

2 tablespoons balsamic vinegar

115g (4oz) small spinach leaves

1 clove garlic, finely crushed

salt and freshly ground black pepper

1 Make the dressing at least 2 hours in advance if possible. Whisk all the ingredients together.

2 Shortly before serving, separate the chicory leaves, then tear them into bite-sized pieces; if you cut them the cut surfaces will discolour.

3 Toss the chicory and spinach with the dressing.

Marinated Grilled Vegetable Salad

*A*LL the vegetables except the peppers can be cooked on a char-grill pan if you like, which will give them an attractive tram-line appearance.

SERVES 6

6 spring onions

1 red pepper, halved lengthways

1 yellow pepper, halved lengthways

1 aubergine, sliced lengthways

2 courgettes, sliced lengthways

12 asparagus spears (optional)

virgin olive oil, for brushing

MARINADE

8 tablespoons extra virgin olive oil

1 tablespoon sherry vinegar

1 clove garlic, finely crushed

1 shallot, diced

1 red chilli, seeded and finely diced

8 basil leaves, torn into shreds

salt and freshly ground black pepper

1 Preheat the grill. Blanch the spring onions in boiling water for 2 minutes. Drain, refresh under running cold water and dry thoroughly.

2 Grill the peppers until charred and blistered all over. Leave until cool enough to handle. Brush the aubergine and courgette slices, spring onions and asparagus spears, if using, with virgin olive oil. Grill until flecked with brown.

3 Remove the skin from the peppers and cut each piece lengthways in half. Put all the vegetables in a non-metallic dish.

4 To make the marinade, mix all the ingredients together. Pour over the vegetables, stir lightly to mix, then cover and leave in a cool place, preferably not the refrigerator, overnight.

Beetroot Salad

*I*F you are not cooking the beetroot yourself, make sure you buy ones that have just been cooked and have not been preserved in vinegar. Small cooked beetroot are now available in vacuum packs.

SERVES 6

700g (1½lb) small cooked beetroot

2 red onions

DRESSING

1 teaspoon caraway seeds

½–1 tablespoon olive oil

1 tablespoon virgin olive oil

1 teaspoon wholegrain mustard

a small bunch of coriander, chopped

75g (3oz) feta cheese

6 tablespoons balsamic vinegar

a dash of Tabasco (optional)

coarse sea salt and freshly ground black pepper

1 Pound the caraway seeds with the ½–1 tablespoon olive oil. Mix with the virgin olive oil, mustard, balsamic vinegar and a dash of Tabasco, if liked. Season to taste.

2 Thinly slice some of the beetroot and cut the remainder into 1cm (½ inch) dice. Pour the dressing over the beetroot and leave to marinate for at least 30 minutes.

3 Just before serving, thinly slice some of the onion and finely chop the remainder. Mix with the beetroot and most of the coriander. Crumble the feta cheese over the salad and scatter with the remaining coriander.

Avocado with Pesto

*T*HE simplicity and speed with which this salad is put together belies its effectiveness.

50ml (2fl oz) virgin olive oil
75g (3oz) pesto

2 avocados, cut into 2.5cm (1 inch) chunks
150g (5oz) mixed salad leaves

1 Stir the oil into the pesto. Stir into the avocados.

2 Put the salad leaves into a bowl, toss in the avocados and serve.

Fennel and Tomato Salad

*W*HEN I am not serving this pretty salad at the same meal as a cheese fondue, I shave 50g (2oz) fresh Parmesan cheese over it.

6 small fennel bulbs, thinly sliced across the grain
2 tablespoons balsamic vinegar
1 clove garlic, crushed
4 tablespoons virgin olive oil

450g (1lb) ripe well-flavoured tomatoes, sliced
115g (4oz) good black olives
salt and freshly ground black pepper

1 Spread the fennel slices in a shallow serving dish.

2 Mix together the vinegar, garlic, oil and seasoning. Pour over the fennel and leave for 20–30 minutes.

3 Scatter the tomatoes over the fennel, then add the olives.

Roast Fennel and Artichoke Salad

OIL left over from the artichokes can be used for salad dressings, tossing with pasta or brushing over vegetables or poultry that are to be grilled or baked.

SERVES 4

4 small fennel bulbs

3 heads of chicory

2 bulbs of garlic, peeled

400g (14oz) jar of artichokes in oil

1 tablespoon sun-dried tomato paste

115g (4oz) herb-flavoured green olives

1 tablespoon pine nuts, toasted

a bunch of coriander, chopped

salt and freshly ground black pepper

1 Preheat the oven to 240°C/475°F/Gas Mark 9. Cut each fennel, chicory and garlic bulb into six.

2 Drain the artichokes, reserving the oil. Cut the artichokes into halves.

3 Mix all the vegetables together with 4–5 tablespoons of the artichoke oil and spread in a shallow, ovenproof dish. Cook in the oven for 15 minutes, then place under the grill for 5–6 minutes to brown.

4 Season and stir well. Transfer to a warm, large, shallow serving dish. Dot the sun-dried tomato paste over the vegetables and scatter with the olives, pine nuts and coriander.

Baked Potato Wedges

*I*F you would prefer to have smaller pieces of potato, cut across the middle of each wedge after it is cooked.

SERVES 4

4 baking potatoes, each weighing about 225g (½lb)

2 tablespoons olive oil

sea salt and freshly ground black pepper

1 Slice each potato into eight equal wedges, put in a large bowl and cover with cold water. Leave for 15 minutes.

2 Preheat the oven to 220°C/425°F/Gas Mark 7. Oil two baking sheets.

3 Drain the potatoes and dry them thoroughly with paper towels. Put into a bowl, pour over the olive oil, add the seasoning and stir together.

4 Spread the potato wedges in a single layer on the baking sheets. Bake for 40 minutes until soft in the centre and brown on the outside. You will need to use two oven shelves, so switch the baking sheets half-way through cooking so that the potatoes cook and colour evenly.

BREADS

Parmesan Cake

*T*HE semolina gives this cheesy, light spongy cake a pleasantly different grainy texture. For my money, the only possible alternative to Parmesan cheese freshly grated from a piece is freshly grated pecorino cheese. Add 1-1½ tablespoons chopped fresh herbs, if liked.

SERVES 4–6 WITH OTHER DIPPERS

75g (3oz) self-raising flour

scant ½ teaspoon baking powder

40g (1½oz) freshly grated Parmesan
    cheese

40g (1½oz) semolina

2 eggs, separated

50g (2oz) unsalted butter, melted

115ml (4fl oz) milk

freshly ground black pepper

1 Preheat the oven to 190°C/375°F/Gas Mark 5. Sift the flour and baking powder into a bowl. Mix in the Parmesan cheese, semolina and pepper. Form a well in the centre, pour in the egg yolks, butter and milk and gradually stir the dry ingredients into the liquids to make a smooth batter.

2 Whisk the egg whites until stiff but not dry. Using a large metal spoon, fold the egg whites into the batter in three or four batches.

3 Pour into a 17.5 × 27.5cm (7 × 11 inch) cake tin lined with greaseproof paper. Bake for 25–30 minutes until the cake is golden and a skewer inserted into the centre comes out clean.

4 Put the cake tin on a wire rack, leave to cool for about 5 minutes, then unmould the cake on to the rack, carefully peel off the paper and leave to cool.

Corn and Chilli Mini Muffins

*T*HESE muffins can be flavoured with finely chopped spring onions or chopped herbs instead of chilli. If more convenient, they can be made in advance and frozen, then reheated in a moderate oven for about 5–10 minutes.

— MAKES ABOUT 32 MINI MUFFINS; ABOUT 40 MINI-PATTY-PAN SIZE —

175g (6oz) self-raising flour	175g (6oz) mature Cheddar cheese, grated
115g (4oz) fine polenta (cornmeal)	2 eggs, lightly beaten
50g (2oz) corn kernels	100–115ml (3½–4fl oz) milk or water
1–2 fresh red chillies, seeded and finely chopped	salt

1 Preheat the oven to 200°C/400°F/Gas Mark 6. Oil or butter the mini-muffin tins or mini-patty pans.

2 Sift the flour and salt into a large bowl and stir in the polenta (cornmeal), corn kernels, chillies and cheese.

3 Make a well in the centre and pour in the eggs and three-quarters of the milk or water. Using a wooden spoon, stir all the ingredients together, adding more milk or water to give a reluctant dropping consistency.

4 Spoon into the prepared tins so that they are full, then bake for 15–20 minutes until well risen and golden. Serve freshly baked.

Soda Bread

*T*HIS is a moist, close-textured loaf that is delicious when eaten still warm from the oven: pull it into small pieces rather than cutting it into cubes. Stoneground flour gives it a really good flavour. (It differs from other flours in that it is ground between stones rather than steel rollers. This means the grains are crushed slowly without stripping away the vitamin-rich wheatgerm.) If you cannot find stoneground flour (it is available in good supermarkets) use Granary or wholemeal. I include a small proportion of white flour to lighten the texture slightly. Buttermilk used to be a by-product of butter-making – it is the liquid that remains after the butter has been churned. It is now made commercially, but if you are unable to find it, use two-thirds semi-skimmed milk and one-third low-fat plain yogurt.

MAKES 1 LARGE ROUND LOAF

450g (1lb) plain stoneground flour

115g (4oz) plain white flour

1 teaspoon bicarbonate of soda

50g (2oz) rolled oats (optional)

about 500ml (18fl oz) buttermilk

salt and freshly ground black pepper

1 Preheat the oven to 230°C/450°F/Gas Mark 8. Sift the flours and bicarbonate of soda into a large bowl, then tip in the contents of the sieve. Stir in the oats, if using, and the seasoning. Make a well in the centre. Pour in the buttermilk and, using your hand, quickly and lightly draw the dry ingredients into the liquid, adding more buttermilk if necessary to make a soft, slightly sticky dough: do not overwork the dough or it will be heavy.

2 Turn the dough on to a lightly floured surface and quickly shape it into a large circle. Put on an oiled baking sheet. Cut a deep cross in the top using a large, sharp knife.

3 Bake the loaf for 15 minutes, then lower the oven temperature to 200°C/400°F/Gas Mark 6 and bake for a further 20–25 minutes until the underside sounds hollow when rapped with the knuckles.

4 Serve while still warm.

Olive Oil Bread

*T*HIS is my standard bread recipe and makes a good reliable bread that comes in very handy for dipping into fondues.

MAKES 1 LOAF

450g (1lb) strong plain flour
1 sachet easy-blend yeast

4 tablespoons virgin olive oil, plus extra for brushing
salt and freshly ground black pepper

1 Sift the flour into the bowl of a food mixer or food processor. Stir in the yeast and seasoning. Add the 4 tablespoons virgin olive oil. With the motor running, slowly pour in about 225ml (8fl oz) water. Continue to mix for 6–8 minutes until the dough is firm and elastic.

2 Turn the dough on to a floured surface and knead into a ball. Put the ball into a large oiled bowl (if you have used a food mixer, you can use that bowl), turn the dough over so that it is coated with oil, then put the bowl inside a large polythene bag or cover it with cling film. Leave at room temperature or in the refrigerator until doubled in volume.

3 Turn the dough on to a floured work surface and punch it down. Form the dough into a fat, squat sausage shape and put on an oiled baking sheet. Brush the top gently with olive oil, cover loosely with oiled cling film and leave until risen and springy.

4 Preheat the oven to 230°C/450°F/Gas Mark 8.

5 Bake the loaf for 10 minutes, then lower the heat to 190°C/375°F/Gas Mark 5 and bake for a further 45 minutes or so until it is golden on top and the underside sounds hollow when rapped with the knuckles.

Herb Bread

*U*SE white, stoneground, Granary or wholemeal flour as you prefer.

MAKES 1 LOAF

450g (1lb) strong flour

1 sachet easy-blend yeast

1 clove garlic, crushed and finely chopped (optional)

2 tablespoons chopped parsley

2 tablespoons chopped mixed herbs such as rosemary (finely chopped), thyme, mint, chives, basil, tarragon

olive oil, for brushing

coarse sea salt, for sprinkling

salt and freshly ground black pepper

1 Sift the flour into the bowl of a food mixer or food processor. Stir in the yeast, garlic, if using, and seasoning. With the motor running, slowly pour in about 300ml (½ pint) water. Continue to mix for 6–8 minutes until the dough is firm and elastic.

2 Turn the dough on to a floured surface and work in the herbs. Form into a ball. Put the ball into a large oiled bowl (if you have used a food mixer, you can use that bowl), turn the dough over so that it is coated with oil, then put the bowl inside a large polythene bag or cover it with cling film. Leave at room temperature or in the refrigerator until doubled in volume.

3 Turn the dough on to the floured work surface and punch it down. Form the dough into a loaf shape and put on an oiled baking sheet. Brush the top gently with olive oil, cover loosely with oiled cling film and leave at room temperature or in the refrigerator until risen and springy.

4 Preheat the oven to 220°C/425°F/Gas Mark 7.

5 Sprinkle coarse sea salt over the top of the loaf. Bake for about 25 minutes until it is golden on top and the underside sounds hollow when rapped with the knuckles.

Parsnip Bread

⟲

*P*ARSNIPS add moistness to the loaf and give it a slight nutty sweetness that marries well with the Granary flour.

— MAKES 1 LOAF —

450g (1lb) parsnips, cut into chunks
40g (1½oz) butter
450g (1lb) Granary flour
1 sachet easy-blend yeast

225ml (8fl oz) milk, plus extra for brushing
2 tablespoons cracked wheat
salt and freshly ground black pepper

1 Boil the parsnips until tender but not too soft, then drain very well. Purée the parsnips with the butter.

2 Sift the flour into the bowl of a food mixer or food processor. Stir in the parsnips, yeast and seasoning. With the motor running, slowly pour in the milk. Continue to mix for 6–8 minutes until the dough is firm and elastic.

3 Turn the dough on to a floured surface and knead into a ball. Put the ball into a large oiled bowl (if you have used a food mixer, you can use that bowl), turn the dough over so that it is coated with oil, then put the bowl inside a large polythene bag or cover it with cling film. Leave at room temperature or in the refrigerator until doubled in volume.

4 Turn the dough on to the floured work surface and punch it down. Form the dough into a loaf shape and put on an oiled baking sheet. Brush the top gently with a little milk and sprinkle with the cracked wheat. Cover loosely with oiled cling film and leave until risen and springy.

5 Preheat the oven to 200°C/400°F/Gas Mark 6.

6 Bake the loaf for about 35 minutes until it is golden on top and the underside sounds hollow when rapped with the knuckles.

Spiced Breadsticks

*T*HE breadsticks should be crisp after they have cooled.

MAKES ABOUT 32

450g (1lb) strong plain flour	50g (2oz) butter, chopped
1 sachet easy-blend yeast	1 egg, beaten
1 teaspoon ground cumin	2 tablespoons cumin seeds
2 tablespoons groundnut (peanut) oil	3 tablespoons sesame seeds
2 tablespoons sesame oil	salt and freshly ground black pepper

1 Sift the flour into the bowl of a food mixer or food processor. Stir in the yeast, ground cumin and seasoning.

2 Put the groundnut and sesame oils into a small saucepan, add the butter and heat gently until the butter has melted.

3 With the food processor or food mixer motor running, slowly pour in the oil mixture and about 200ml (7fl oz) water. Continue to mix for 6–8 minutes until the dough is firm and elastic.

4 Turn the dough on to a floured surface and knead into a ball. Put the ball into a large oiled bowl (if you have used a food mixer, you can use that bowl), turn the dough over so that it is coated with oil, then put the bowl inside a large polythene bag or cover it with cling film. Leave at room temperature or in the refrigerator until doubled in volume.

5 Turn the dough on to the floured work surface and punch it down. Divide into 32 pieces. Roll each piece to a sausage shape about 20cm (8 inches) long. Transfer to oiled baking sheets. Brush the sticks with beaten egg. Mix together the cumin and sesame seeds and sprinkle evenly over the sticks. Cover and leave for about 20–25 minutes.

6 Preheat the oven to 200°C/400°F/Gas Mark 6. Bake the breadsticks for 15–20 minutes until golden brown. Turn off the oven and leave the breadsticks to cool in the oven.

Sun-Dried Tomato and Basil Focaccia

*I*N place of, or as well as, the sun-dried tomatoes, try adding chopped black olives that have been packed in oil, and chopped anchovy fillets.

MAKES 1 LARGE LOAF

50g (2oz) sun-dried tomatoes in olive oil, drained and chopped, the oil reserved

200ml (7fl oz) boiling water

450g (1lb) strong plain flour

1 sachet easy-blend yeast

1 egg, beaten

4 tablespoons mixed oils from the sun-dried tomatoes and olive oil

4 tablespoons chopped basil

olive oil, for brushing

salt and freshly ground black pepper

1 Put the sun-dried tomatoes into a bowl and pour over the water. Leave for 15 minutes. Drain off the water and reserve.

2 Sift the flour into the bowl of a food mixer or food processor. Stir in the yeast and seasoning. With the motor running, slowly pour in the reserved water, the egg and the mixed oils. Continue to mix for 6–8 minutes until the dough is firm and elastic.

3 Turn the dough on to a floured surface and work in the sun-dried tomatoes and basil. Form into a ball. Put the ball into a large oiled bowl (if you have used a food mixer, you can use that bowl), turn the dough over so that it is coated with oil, then put the bowl inside a large polythene bag. Leave at room temperature or in the refrigerator until doubled in volume.

4 Turn the dough on to the floured work surface and punch it down. Press into a 2.5cm (1 inch) thick square approximately 25cm (10 inches) across. Put on an oiled baking sheet. Using the handle of a wooden spoon or a finger, make deep indentations over the surface. Brush generously with olive oil. Leave until risen and springy. Indent again, if necessary.

5 Preheat the oven to 200°C/400°F/Gas Mark 6.

6 Bake the loaf for about 25 minutes until it is golden on top and the underside sounds hollow when rapped with the knuckles.

Naan Bread

*I*F you would prefer to make the naan in advance, leave them to cool, then wrap them in a polythene bag. Before the meal, wrap each one in foil and heat in the oven at 200°C/400°F/Gas Mark 6 for about 15 minutes.

MAKES ABOUT 8

225g (8oz) self-raising flour | about 150ml (5fl oz) plain yogurt
paprika, to taste | salt and freshly ground black pepper

1 Sift the flour into a large bowl and stir in the paprika and seasonings. Work with your fingers and slowly add as much yogurt as you need to make a soft, slightly sticky and resilient dough. Turn on to a work surface and knead for about 10 minutes.

2 Put the dough into a bowl, cover with a damp cloth and leave in a warm place to ferment for about 1 hour.

3 Preheat the grill and a griddle or heavy frying pan.

4 Knead the dough briefly then, with floured fingers, break off an egg-sized piece of dough. (Keep the remaining dough covered.) Form into a ball and roll out on an unfloured surface to an oval 20–23cm (8–9 inches) long and 8mm (¹/₃ inch) thick.

5 Slap the bread on to the hot griddle or frying pan and cook until it is completely or partly puffed up, then put under the grill until the puffing up is complete and the bread is speckled with brown patches. Remove, brush with butter, if liked, and stack to keep hot while cooking the remaining naan.

Walnut Bread

*T*HIS makes a good nutty-flavoured loaf that complements cheese fondues well. Cooking the nuts until they are crisp intensifies their flavour.

MAKES 2 LOAVES

600g (1lb 6oz) strong plain flour
1 sachet easy-blend yeast
3 tablespoons walnut oil

150g (5oz) walnuts, cooked in the oven or under the grill until crisp, chopped
salt and freshly ground black pepper

1 Sift the flour into the bowl of a food mixer or food processor. Stir in the yeast and seasoning. Add the walnut oil. With the motor running, slowly pour in about 350ml (12fl oz) water. Continue to mix for 6–8 minutes until the dough is firm and elastic.

2 Turn the dough on to a floured surface and work in the walnuts. Form the dough into a ball. Put the ball into a large oiled bowl (if you have used a food mixer, you can use that bowl), turn the dough over so that it is coated with oil, then put the bowl inside a large polythene bag or cover it with cling film. Leave at room temperature or in the refrigerator until doubled in volume.

3 Turn the dough on to the floured work surface and punch it down. Divide in half and form each piece into a roll about 20cm (8 inches) long. Place on separate oiled baking sheets. Slash each loaf top three times with a sharp knife. Cover with lightly oiled cling film and leave until doubled in size and springy.

4 Preheat the oven to 220°C/425°F/Gas Mark 7.

5 Bake the loaves for 12 minutes. Lower the oven temperature to 180°C/350°F/Gas Mark 4 and bake for a further 25 minutes until they are golden on top and the undersides sound hollow when rapped with the knuckles.

6 Leave to cool for a few minutes then turn on to a wire rack. Serve warm.

Potato and Chive Bread

*M*ASHED potato produces a loaf with a moist texture, a subtle but discernibly different taste and good keeping qualities.

MAKES 3 LOAVES

450g (1lb) potatoes

150ml (5fl oz) milk, plus extra for brushing

25g (1oz) butter

700g (1½lb) strong white flour

1 sachet easy-blend yeast

a large bunch of chives, chopped

salt and freshly ground black pepper

1 Boil the potatoes until tender. Drain well then return to the saucepan and put over a very low heat to dry off slightly. Beat in the milk and butter. Leave to cool.

2 Sift the flour into the bowl of a food mixer or food processor. Stir in the yeast and seasoning. Add the potatoes. With the motor running, slowly pour in 425ml (15fl oz) water. Continue to mix for 6–8 minutes until the dough is firm and elastic.

3 Turn the dough on to a floured surface and knead into a ball. Put the ball into a large oiled bowl (if you have used a food mixer, you can use that bowl), turn the dough over so that it is coated with oil, then put the bowl inside a large polythene bag or cover it with cling film. Leave at room temperature or in the refrigerator until doubled in volume.

4 Turn the dough on to the floured work surface. Punch it down and work in the chives. Form the dough into three loaves. Brush the tops gently with milk, cover and leave until risen and springy.

5 Preheat the oven to 220°C/425°F/Gas Mark 7.

6 Bake the loaves for 10 minutes. Lower the oven temperature to 190°C/375°F/Gas Mark 5 and bake for a further 25 minutes or until golden on top and the undersides sound hollow when rapped with the knuckles.

CAKES AND BISCUITS

Madeleines

*T*HESE delicate, shell-shaped French madeleines are baked in special tins; I have found that 7.5cm (3 inch) ones produce the best results. Serve freshly baked, if possible.

MAKES ABOUT 20

3 eggs, separated	90g (3½oz) plain flour
90g (3½oz) caster sugar	grated rind of 1 large lemon
90g (3½oz) unsalted butter, melted	1½ tablespoons lemon juice
1 scant teaspoon baking powder	icing sugar, for dusting

1 Whisk the egg yolks with the sugar until thick and pale yellow, then slowly stir in the melted butter.

2 Whisk the egg whites until stiff but not dry, then, using a large metal spoon, carefully fold them into the egg yolk mixture in batches, alternating with the baking powder and flour sifted over the surface.

3 Finally, fold in the lemon rind and juice. Refrigerate the mixture for 30 minutes.

4 Meanwhile, preheat the oven to 225°C/425°F/Gas Mark 7 and butter and flour the madeleine moulds generously.

5 Spoon the cake mixture into the moulds so that they are two-thirds full, and bake for about 7 minutes, until domed, then lower the oven temperature to 190°C/375°F/Gas Mark 5 and bake for a further 7 minutes or so until pale golden brown on top and slightly darker brown around the edges.

6 Run the tip of a knife around the edges of each madeleine and unmould on to a wire rack. Dust with icing sugar.

Sponge Fingers

◉

SPONGE fingers are very easy to make at home and far superior to shop-bought ones.

MAKES 20

4 eggs

100g (3½oz) caster sugar

65g (2½oz) plain flour

15g (½oz) arrowroot or cornflour

1 Preheat the oven to 200°C/400°F/Gas Mark 6. Line 2 large baking sheets with baking parchment. Draw parallel lines 12.5cm (5 inches) apart on the paper.

2 Separate three of the eggs. Beat the yolks with the whole egg and most of the caster sugar until very pale.

3 Whisk the egg whites until stiff, then whisk in the remaining caster sugar. Using a large metal spoon, gently fold into the egg yolk mixture in three batches.

4 Mix the flour and arrowroot or cornflour together, then sift them over the egg yolk mixture and carefully fold in.

5 Spoon into a piping bag fitted with a 5mm (¼ inch) plain nozzle and pipe 7.5–10cm (3–4 inch) long fingers along using the drawn lines.

6 Bake on the top and middle shelves of the oven for about 10 minutes until lightly browned; switch the baking sheets around half-way through baking.

7 Invert the fingers on to a clean tea-towel. Immediately and carefully peel off the baking parchment. Transfer the sponge fingers to a wire rack to cool.

Langues de Chat

LONG, delicately crisp langues de chat are ideal for dipping into sweet fondues.

MAKES 30–40

100g (3½oz) butter, softened

100g (3½oz) caster sugar

3 egg whites, lightly whisked

100g (3½oz) self-raising flour

---

1 Preheat the oven to 200°C/400°F/Gas Mark 6. Grease two or three large baking sheets. Beat the butter and sugar together until light and fluffy.

2 Gradually beat in the egg whites.

3 Sift the flour over the surface of the butter mixture, then gently fold in until just evenly mixed.

4 Spoon the mixture into a piping bag fitted with a 1cm (½ inch) plain nozzle. Pipe into fingers the thickness of a pencil and about 5 cm (2 inches) long, on the baking sheets. Bake for about 8 minutes until lightly browned in the centre and brown at the edges.

5 Cool the biscuits slightly, then transfer to a wire rack using a fish slice or palette knife. Leave to cool completely. Store in an airtight container.

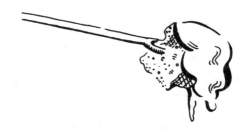

Sponge Cake

❂

*T*HIS is the basic cake recipe that is the foundation of so many cakes, including the Victoria sandwich; here it is baked in a rectangular tin to make it easier to cut it into neat pieces. The keys to a light, delicate, well-flavoured cake are using good, unsalted butter, large eggs and beating the mixture well in Steps 2 and 3; an electric whisk or a food mixer are a real boon. For the cake to be at its best, eat on the day of baking, or make it in advance, freeze until the day it is required, then thaw in the refrigerator.

———————————— SERVES 4 ————————————

115g (4oz) unsalted butter, softened, plus extra for greasing

115g (4oz) caster sugar, preferably vanilla-flavoured

2 large eggs

115g (4oz) self-raising flour

1 Preheat the oven to 180°C/350°F/Gas Mark 4. Butter a 22.5 × 27.5 cm (9 × 11 inch) cake tin and line the base with greaseproof paper cut to fit.

2 Beat the butter and sugar together until light and fluffy.

3 Gradually beat the eggs into the butter mixture, beating well after each addition.

4 Sift half the flour over the beaten mixture and fold in gently until almost combined, using a large metal spoon. Repeat with the remaining flour, folding it in until just evenly combined.

5 Turn into the tin, smooth the surface and bake for about 25 minutes until springy in the centre.

6 Leave to cool in the tin for about 5 minutes, then invert on to a wire rack lined with a clean tea-towel and carefully peel off the paper. Leave to cool completely.

Viennese Fingers

VIENNESE fingers have a 'short' texture and are buttery and not too sweet.

115g (4oz) butter
25g (1oz) icing sugar, sifted
115g (4oz) plain flour

¼ teaspoon baking powder
a few drops of vanilla essence

1 Preheat the oven to 190°C/375°F/Gas Mark 5. Grease two or three baking sheets.

2 Beat the butter and icing sugar until light and fluffy. Sift the flour and baking powder over the butter mixture, then gently fold in, adding the vanilla essence as well, until just evenly mixed.

3 Spoon the mixture into a piping bag fitted with a 5mm (¼ inch) star nozzle and pipe twenty-four 5cm (2 inch) fingers on the baking sheets. Bake for 15 minutes.

4 Leave the biscuits to cool for a few minutes, then transfer to a wire rack to cool.

VARIATION
Chocolate Viennese Fingers
Add 2 tablespoons cocoa powder with the flour.

Après-Fondue Desserts

Many people do not feel that they have had a proper meal unless they have had a dessert, yet a fondue, especially a cheese one, can be rich and filling – which poses the question: 'What to serve?' Fruit is the easy, and common, solution and one that will please quite a number of people. But it can leave real dessert-lovers feeling unsatisfied, as if something is missing, and that the meal they have just eaten was inadequate and incomplete. So my way to please everyone is to provide a fruit dessert that is a little special, but not rich.

Melon and Berry Medley

AN attractive and refreshing combination of different-coloured melons and traditional summer berries makes a welcome change of pace after a fondue, particularly a cheese or oil one.

SERVES 4

1 Charentais melon

150ml (5fl oz) fresh orange juice

2 tablespoons melon liqueur or Cointreau

½ ogen or Galia melon

350g (12oz) mixed summer fruits such as strawberries, raspberries, loganberries, blueberries

sprigs of mint, to decorate

TO SERVE

Langues de Chat (see page 140) or Madeleines (see page 138)

Greek yogurt or crème fraîche

1 Halve and seed the Charentais melon. Coarsely chop one half and put in a blender with the orange juice and liqueur. Mix to a purée. Set aside.

2 Discard the seeds from the ogen or Galia melon. Use a melon baller to scoop out the flesh from the remaining Charentais melon and the ogen or Galia melon. If you do not have a melon baller, cut the flesh into cubes.

3 Put the melon flesh into a serving bowl and pour the puréed melon over it. Stir gently.

4 Add the summer fruits to the bowl and stir again to lightly mix the fruits together. Leave at room temperature for at least 30 minutes to allow the flavours to mature.

5 To serve, decorate with small sprigs of mint, and serve with langues de chat or madeleines, and Greek yogurt or crème fraîche.

Baked Apples with a Middle Eastern Flavour

*T*HE special yet simple combination of ingredients in the filling, together with the honey-sweetened, fragrant, buttery juices, give an exotic, luxurious air to an everyday pudding that is hard to resist.

SERVES 6

6 baking apples

40g (1½oz) stoned no-need-to-soak prunes, finely chopped

40g (1½oz) dried figs, finely chopped

40g (1½oz) walnuts, chopped

2 tablespoons finely chopped stem ginger

1 teaspoon finely grated lemon rind

1 tablespoon apricot preserve

¼ teaspoon ground cinnamon

25g (1oz) unsalted butter

115g (4oz) clear honey

75ml (3fl oz) orange juice

1 tablespoon lemon juice

finely crushed seeds from 3 cardamom pods

crème fraîche, Greek yogurt or vanilla ice cream, to serve

1 Preheat the oven to 180°C/350°F/Gas Mark 4.

2 Core the apples and enlarge the cavities. With the point of a sharp knife, score around the circumference of each apple, then put the apples in a shallow baking dish which they will just fit.

3 In a bowl, mix together the prunes, figs, walnuts, ginger, lemon rind, apricot preserve and cinnamon until well combined.

4 Pack the mixture into the cavities in the apples.

5 In a small saucepan, gently heat the butter, honey, orange juice, lemon juice and cardamom seeds, stirring with a wooden spoon until the butter has melted and the mixture is smooth.

6 Pour over the apples and bake for about 45 minutes until the apples are soft, basting every 10 minutes or so.

7 Serve with the cooking juices spooned over and accompanied by crème fraîche, Greek yogurt or ice cream.

Fruit Salad in a Chocolate Bowl

***W*HEN** you want a dessert that will impress, or give a special treat, for hardly any effort, this is the one to choose. For the best flavour and texture make sure all the fruit is ripe.

SERVES 8

2 nectarines, halved, stoned and cut into cubes

4 apricots, halved, stoned and cut into cubes

1 kiwi fruit, peeled and sliced

115g (4oz) blueberries or blackberries

150g (5oz) strawberries, halved if large

1 mango, halved, stoned and cut into cubes

115g (4oz) black cherries, halved and stoned

1 Charentais melon

1 papaya

3 passion fruit

225g (8oz) raspberries

eau-de-vie de framboise or cognac, to taste (optional)

icing sugar, to taste

crème fraîche or Greek yogurt, to serve

CHOCOLATE BOWL

225g (8oz) good-quality chocolate

flavourless oil, for brushing

1 To make the chocolate bowl, grate the chocolate into a heat-proof bowl placed over a saucepan of hot, but not boiling, water. Leave until melted, stirring occasionally.

2 Meanwhile, line a glass bowl that will take the fruit comfortably with foil, pressing it firmly into the shape of the bowl and smoothing it as flat as possible. Brush lightly with oil.

3 Using a large pastry brush, paint an even layer of chocolate on the foil to cover it completely. Leave until set hard. Repeat until all the chocolate has been used.

4 Put the nectarines, apricots, kiwi fruit, berries, mango and cherries in a bowl.

5 Halve the melon, scoop out and discard the seeds. Using a melon baller, scoop the flesh into the bowl. Do the same with the papaya.

6 Halve the passion fruit and scoop the seeds into the bowl.

7 Put the raspberries in a blender and mix to a purée. Pass through a non-metallic sieve and add *eau-de-vie* or cognac and icing sugar, to taste. Pour over the fruit in the bowl then, using a large spoon, lightly stir the fruits together.

8 To serve, ease the chocolate-covered foil from the glass bowl, then very carefully peel off the foil. Put the chocolate bowl on a serving plate. Fill with the fruit, and serve with crème fraîche or Greek yogurt.

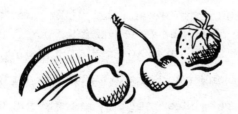

Honeycomb Plum Mousse

❧

*T*HIS airy plum mousse, which is spiked with cardamom, separates into two layers when unmoulded to show a clear top and a fluffy lower section.

SERVES 4–6

450g (1lb) ripe red plums, halved and stoned

115ml (4fl oz) fresh orange juice

75g (3oz) caster sugar

$\frac{1}{2}$–$\frac{3}{4}$ teaspoon finely ground, toasted cardamom seeds

3 teaspoons gelatine

2 egg whites

1 Put the plums, 2 tablespoons of the orange juice, the sugar and cardamom seeds in a saucepan. Heat gently, stirring gently occasionally, until the sugar has dissolved and the plum juices are starting to run. Increase the heat slightly so that the mixture is just bubbling, and leave to cook until the plums are very soft. Leave to cool slightly.

2 Pour the remaining orange juice into a small bowl and sprinkle the gelatine over it. Leave until spongy, then put the bowl over a saucepan of hot water until the gelatine has melted. Cool slightly.

3 When the plum mixture and the gelatine mixture have both reached approximately the same warm temperature, slowly pour the gelatine into the plum mixture, stirring thoroughly.

4 Pour into a blender and mix to a purée. Leave to cool.

5 Whisk the egg whites until they are stiff but not dry. Stir 2 tablespoons of the egg whites into the plum mixture, then, using a large metal spoon, gently fold in the remainder in three batches, until just evenly mixed.

6 Spoon the mixture into a jelly mould and leave in the refrigerator for several hours until the mousse is set.

7 To serve, very briefly dip the mould in hot water, invert a serving plate on top of the mould, then turn the two over together. Lift the mould away.

Hot Rum-Buttered Pineapple

*W*HITE rum makes a lighter dessert than dark rum. For extra zip, add some cinnamon, cardamom or freshly grated ginger.

───────── SERVES 6 ─────────

115g (4oz) unsalted butter

75g (3oz) soft dark brown sugar

200ml (7fl oz) white rum

juice and finely grated rind of 1 orange

1 medium pineapple, about 1.4kg (3lb)

Greek yogurt, crème fraîche or vanilla ice cream, to serve

1 Put the butter, sugar, rum and orange juice in a large frying pan and heat gently, stirring occasionally, until the sugar has dissolved. Increase the heat, bring to the boil and bubble vigorously for 3 minutes.

2 Meanwhile, peel the pineapple, slice thinly and remove the core from each slice. Add the pineapple slices to the pan in two batches, and cook each batch for about 1 minute.

3 Spoon the hot pineapple with the buttery rum sauce on to warm plates and sprinkle with the orange rind. Serve with spoonfuls of chilled Greek yogurt, crème fraîche or vanilla ice cream.

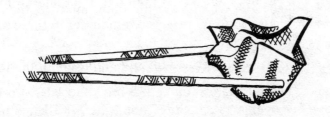

Adult Orange Jelly with Chocolate Thins

*F*ORGET about orange jelly from a packet. This jelly, made with shop-bought freshly squeezed orange juice (*not* long-life orange juice from a carton) has a definite fruity taste, which I complement with wafer-thin squares, or other shapes, of bitter, dark chocolate. The jelly is best eaten on the day it is made because the gelatine can toughen if left to stand for longer; however, the chocolate thins can be made several days ahead.

SERVES 6

1 litre (1¾pints) fresh orange juice   15g (½oz) gelatine

CHOCOLATE THINS

about 175g (6oz) good-quality plain chocolate

1 Rinse a jelly mould with cold water, pour out the water and leave the mould upside-down to drain.

2 Pour 4 tablespoons of the orange juice into a small bowl. Sprinkle the gelatine over it and leave to soak until spongy. Put the bowl over a saucepan of hot water until the gelatine has dissolved. Set aside to cool slightly.

3 Gently warm half the remaining orange juice until it is approximately the same temperature as the gelatine mixture. Remove from the heat and slowly pour in the gelatine mixture, stirring constantly.

4 Pour in the remaining juice, then pour into the prepared mould. Leave in the refrigerator for several hours until set.

5 To make the chocolate thins, grate the chocolate into a heat-proof bowl set over a saucepan of hot water and leave to melt, stirring occasionally. When the chocolate is smooth, spread it in a thin, even layer on non-stick baking parchment. Leave until almost set.

6 With a sharp knife, mark the chocolate into shapes such as squares, rectangles, fingers or diamonds. Leave to set completely, then cut out the chocolate shapes along the marked lines.

7 To serve the dessert, dip the mould very briefly in hot water, invert a serving plate on top of the mould, then turn the two over together. Shake the mould, then lift it away. Serve with the chocolate thins.

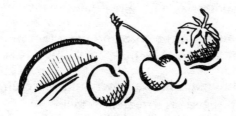

Strawberries with Fragrant Rose Cream

*U*SE petals from roses that have not been sprayed with pesticides or other chemicals for this dessert, which encapsulates the essence of summer. For choice, pick the roses in the morning, after the dew has evaporated but before the sun has become too hot. If you don't have suitably fragrant roses, you can flavour the cream with triple-strength rose-water, and colour it with a few drops of cochineal. If you prefer, you can use all crème fraîche, or light crème fraîche, instead of the single cream and yogurt.

SERVES 6

550g (1¼lb) strawberries	65ml (2½fl oz) crème fraîche
1 fragrant dark red rose	65ml (2½fl oz) Greek yogurt
300ml (½ pint) single cream	caster sugar, to taste

1 Hull the strawberries and halve them.

2 Pick the petals from the rose and put them in a blender. Add the single cream and mix briefly.

3 Pour the rose cream into a bowl, add the créme fraîche and yogurt and whip together. Sweeten to taste.

4 Spoon the rose cream into an attractive glass serving bowl, or individual glass dishes, and spoon the strawberries over the top.

Index

153